TITAN

Belfast's Own

STEPHEN CAMERON is a co-founder and past Chairman of the Belfast Titanic Society, which was formerly called The Ulster Titanic Society. He has researched the *Titanic* since 1992. He was a Station Commander with the Northern Ireland Fire Brigade. He lives in Bangor, Co. Down with his wife. He continues to research the subject and has lectured widely on his research.

This publication is dedicated to the memory of my late father
James W.B. Cameron

TITANIC

Belfast's Own

With best wishes
Stephen Cameron

STEPHEN CAMERON

Published 2011 by
Colourpoint Books
Colourpoint House, Jubilee Business Park
Jubilee Road, Newtownards, BT23 4YH
Tel: 028 9182 6339
Fax: 028 9182 1900
E-mail: info@colourpoint.co.uk
Web: www.colourpoint.co.uk

First Edition
First Impression

Designed by April Sky Design, Newtownards
Tel: 028 9182 7195
Web: www.aprilsky.co.uk

Printed by W&G Baird, Antrim

ISBN 978-1-906578-77-0

Front cover: 'Into the Night' by E.D. Walker

CONTENTS

ACKNOWLEDGEMENTS

Putting together a publication like this cannot be done as a solo effort. Throughout my research, many people have encouraged, directed, advised and just been there when needed. I should like to thank the following for their help:

Ken Anderson and Michael McCaughan of the Ulster Folk and Transport Museum;
The staff at Bangor Library;
The staff at the Public Record Office of Northern Ireland;
Mr M. McComb, Head Librarian, *Belfast Newsletter*;
Mr W. McAuley, Head Librarian, *Belfast Telegraph*;
The relatives of the Ulster men and women who sailed on the *Titanic*, for their assistance and for permitting the invasion of their privacy;
The office-holders and committee of the Ulster *Titanic* Society. The name of the Society was changed in 2003 to The Belfast Titanic Society;
Una Reilly and the late Rupert Millar, John Parkinson, Tommy McBride and Marjorie McCormick of the Belfast Titanic Society;
Harland and Wolff Technical Services Department, especially Mr Jim Lee and Mrs Lorraine Cunningham;
Robert Davis of Wine Inns;
Mr John Leckey, the Belfast Coroner;
David Livingstone, Chris Hackett and the late John Bedford, for technical advice;
Patrick Stenson, for guidance and advice;
Barbara Walker and my daughter Victoria, for planting the seed that spawned my obsession with the *Titanic*;
Seamus Cashman, Eilís French, Emer Ryan and all the staff at Wolfhound Press who were the original publishers of this book;
Malcolm Johnston, Jacky Hawkes, Rachel Irwin and all the staff at Colourpoint Books for the support and advice given with this reprint;
My wife Sylvia and my son Richard, for their encouragement and support.

Picture and Document Acknowledgements

John Andrews
Belfast Newsletter
Belfast Telegraph
Roderick Boggs
Kate Dornan
Harper Memorial Baptist Church
Maureen Howard
Patricia McDonald
Ian McGowan
Institute of Marine Engineers
May Street Presbyterian Church
Rupert Millar
Allison Murphy

Fred Parkes
Marjorie Wilson
Crown copyright material in the Public Record Office of Northern Ireland is reproduced by permission of the Deputy Keeper of Records (Harland and Wolff collection, reference D2805)
The National Archives, ref. BT100/259
Ulster Folk and Transport Museum, Harland and Wolff photographic collection
Ulster Museum photographic collection
Belfast *Titanic* Society
Trustees of National Museums Northern Ireland

For permission to reproduce the copyright material we gratefully acknowledge the above. Copyright has been acknowledged to the best of our ability. If there are any inadvertent errors or omissions, we shall be happy to correct them in any future editions.

FOREWORD

For many people, the tragedy of the *Titanic* seems to hold a timeless fascination — the story of the then largest luxury liner ever made, launched in 1911 and commissioned in 1912, and of the tragic end which befell the ship and many people, so long ago.

For some, the tragedy seemed like the end of an era and perhaps of a different way of life. At the time there was great wealth and luxury, but also considerable poverty and deprivation. Then, only two years after the *Titanic* sank with over 1,500 lives lost, came the horrors of the Great War and the loss of so many lives. On the fields of France and Belgium 1,500 lives could have been lost in an hour or so.

To others, including myself, the memory of the *Titanic* brings another sadness. I think of my relative whose young and promising life was so suddenly cut short, together with the lives of so many other unfortunate people of all classes and creeds, rich and poor, young and old, passengers and crew. My great-uncle — together with all those others who, full of hope, were travelling across the Atlantic on the great ship — never thought that the worst could happen on that fateful night.

My connection with the *Titanic* concerns my great-uncle Thomas. He entered the shipyard of Harland and Wolff as a young boy and worked his way up to become Managing Director. It is recognised that he had a major role in the construction of the *Titanic* and other ships at that time, going back to the end of the last century. Some of these were built for the White Star Line.

Thomas Andrews had crossed the Atlantic several times on the maiden voyages of these other ships. Among the most famous of these were the *Oceanic* and the *Olympic*. This was the reason he was on the maiden voyage of the *Titanic*; he also led the guarantee group from Harland and Wolff.

The last port of call was Queenstown, County Cork, and the ship's final destination was New York.

I recall my father telling the story of how his Uncle Tommy brought him to the launch of the *Titanic* in May 1911. My father, then aged eight, was allowed to help knock away one of the wooden wedges holding the ship on the slipway. He always remembered that day when he had a part in launching 'the big ship that Uncle Tommy had made'.

I was delighted and privileged to be asked to write this introduction. I have known Stephen Cameron for years. When he first approached me about this book, I thought there would be little new information available about the *Titanic*; but he has spent over five years researching the period when the famous vessel was constructed in Belfast, followed by the final disaster, and his meticulous research has uncovered a vast amount of new information.

Stephen has shown great understanding and appreciation of the local people and their stories connected with the *Titanic*, its birthplace, and its final tragic ending.

I wish him and this publication every success.

John M.J. Andrews
President of the Belfast Titanic Society

The Arroll Gantry under which the Olympic and Titanic would be built.

(Ulster Folk and Transport Museum. Photograph reproduced courtesy the Trustees of National Museums Northern Ireland)

CHAPTER 1

Introduction

When the *Titanic* sailed majestically down Belfast Lough in the early evening of 2 April 1912, thousands of people watched her departure from vantage points adjoining the Lough. No one present dreamed that within a few days this ship, then the largest vessel ever to be built, would be at the bottom of the North Atlantic. The crowds had gathered to wish Harland and Wolff's creation good luck; but the *Titanic* was destined not to fulfil the vision of her builders and owners, but to enter the realms of legend.

Since the disaster in 1912, there have been numerous books and films on every aspect of the story of the ship, her passengers and their fate. *A Night to Remember*; *The Night Lives On*; *SOS Titanic*; *Titanic, Triumph and Tragedy*; *Thomas Andrews, Shipbuilder,* James Cameron's Oscar winning film *Titanic* and the excellent ghost story *Something's Alive on the Titanic* are but a few examples of this material.

References to the name 'Titanic' have been made in contexts ranging from a complaint about seating arrangements at the opening sessions of the Forum of Peace and Reconciliation, in Belfast in 1996, to programmes such as the BBC's 'Neighbours' or Granada Television's 'Coronation Street'. The Reverend Pat Buckley has even mentioned the ship in his Sunday column in the *News of the World*.

There are numerous societies all over the world devoted to keeping the story alive. The Belfast Titanic Society's past President was a sprightly man in his nineties who witnessed the *Titanic* leaving Belfast for the last time on 2 April 1912. Other members of this society — of which I am current secretary and historian — include workmen from the Harland and Wolff shipyard, where the *Titanic* was built, and relatives of those lost.

With this intense interest, there can be very few people in the civilised world who are not aware of the *Titanic*. You have only to walk past the bars in the Spanish Costas and eventually you will find a Titanic Bar. In America there is even a town called Titanic.

The amount of knowledge gathered on the subject appears to be never-ending. Even today, eighty-five years on, there is still heated debate on subjects like the quality of the steel used in the ship's hull plates, or the removal of items from the wreck site, or the saga of what Captain Lord of the *Californian* did, or did not do, that night. Passenger and crew lists have been drawn up, and much has been written about the rich and famous people on board.

One area, however, has largely been overlooked: the story of the place where the *Titanic* spent the longest period of time (apart from the spot where she now rests) — her time of construction and fitting-out. That place is Belfast. I should point out here that my research into the *Titanic* is centred on her time in Belfast, and those local people who both worked and sailed on her. The use of the term Ulster in this work denotes that area of the island — present-day Northern Ireland. In 1912 Ireland was one, but my primary aim is to ensure that the story of the people from this area alone is fully told. I know that the Irish *Titanic* Historical Society, which is based in Dublin, is currently engaged in researching and perpetuating the memory of the *Titanic* with regard to the remainder of Ireland, which would also include Donegal, Cavan and Monaghan.

In this publication, I do not intend to retell the *Titanic*'s story. This has been extremely well documented in those publications previously mentioned, and others such as *Titanic: An Illustrated History* or the excellent educational pack available from the Ulster Folk and Transport Museum at Cultra, Holywood. I intend to look at the events in the city of her birth — Belfast — from the time of the *Titanic*'s conception through the time when Belfast and Ulster mourned the loss of their loved ones and their *Titanic*. These events have never before been described in full. This publication provides a new insight into the continuing story of the *SS Titanic*.

The chairman of the Irish *Titanic* Historical Society, Mr Ed Coghlan, once explained to me that he felt the *Titanic* story was like a bicycle wheel, with the ship at the hub and the various stories radiating outwards like the spokes of the wheel. I hope I have added a new spoke to that wheel.[1]

CHAPTER 2

The Construction of SS 401

The partnership between Edward Harland and Gustav Wolff, whose joint venture was to become the massive Belfast shipyard on the east side of the River Lagan, began in April 1861.

Edward Harland was born in Scarborough in 1831, the son of a doctor and part-time engineer. Obviously, his father's interest in things mechanical rubbed off on the young Edward, and at the age of fifteen he entered the engineering works of Robert Stephenson and Company in Newcastle-upon-Tyne. He became involved with the shipbuilding that was taking place on the River Clyde, and in 1854 he moved to Belfast and joined Robert Hickson's new shipyard at Queens Island. Within four years, he bought Hickson out, and at the age of twenty-seven, Harland was the proud owner of his own shipbuilding yard.

In April 1857, on the advice of his uncle, Harland took on Gustav Wolff as a personal assistant. Wolff had been born in Germany in 1835 and had a background in engineering. In 1861, Wolff was taken on as a partner, and in January 1862 the company's name was changed to Harland and Wolff.

The yard has continued to build ships ever since and, to date, it has built over 1,500 vessels. However, with the decline in British shipbuilding, no ship has been built at the shipyard since the launch of the *Anvil Point* in 2003.

In July 1908, the White Star Line of Liverpool gave Harland and Wolff a contract to build three massive ships, to be known as the Olympic-class liners. The second of the three was to become perhaps the most famous ship built since Noah's Ark. She was called *Titanic*.

* * *

In the early years of the twentieth century, life in the Harland and Wolff shipyard was hard. The working day started just after 6.00 a.m. and went on until 5.30 p.m., with only Saturday afternoon and Sunday off. The managers were expected to be at their posts before 6.00 a.m. to supervise the start of the day. The workmen needed to bring two lots of food with them — something for breakfast, normally taken at 8.30 a.m., and something for lunch, which was at 1.00 p.m. Many a young boy would have to run after a father late for work to give his da his 'piece'.

One way to be sure of employment in the shipyard was to join the company as a premium apprentice. The families of young boys would pay Harland and Wolff a fee, which could be anything up to £100. This ensured that if the young apprentice could prove his worth, he could look forward to a possible good promotion when his apprenticeship ended. Thomas Andrews and Saxon Payne both entered the shipyard this way. Andrews reached the position of chief designer, and Payne was made responsible for the Belfast works.

Boys were also taken on at an early age — some as young as fourteen — to serve a normal apprenticeship, usually for a period of five years. The apprentice normally had to supply his own tools, and a lot of hard saving was done; the journeyman to whom the boy was apprenticed would also contribute towards the cost. When the tools were finally bought, the first thing the apprentice would do was to have his name stamped on them. Once bought, these tools were never let out of their owner's sight.

Union card for John Livingstone McGowan, an iron turner employed at Harland and Wolff, August 1910.

(Ian McGowan)

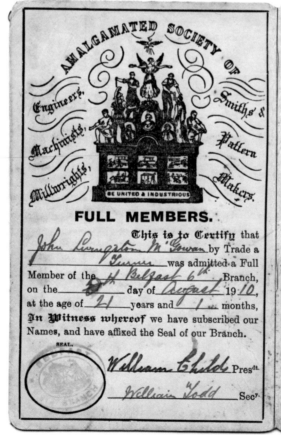

ENGINE WORKS, STAFF WAGES, WEEK ENDING 25th April 1912

NAME		Friday	Saturday	Monday	Tuesday	Wedsday	Thursday	AMOUNT		OBSERVATIONS
— Foremen —										
W. Roy	Boilermaker							5	5	
I. Blackwood	do							3	10	
A. Frost	Fitter							4	5	
R. Adair	Erector							4	·	
I. Fox	do							4	·	
I. M'Dougall	Turner							4	·	
A. M'Kay	Machineman							3	10	
G. Kelly	Smith							4	·	
S. Steele	Patternmaker							3	10	
W. Smith	Brass Finisher							3	10	
I. Cotter	Iron Moulder							5	5	
W. Baxter	do							3	10	
H. O'Neill	Brass Moulder							3	15	
A. M'Diarmid	Coppersmith							4	5	
							£	56	5	0

Yard closed one day (illness reasons)

Week ending 2nd May 1912

NAME		Friday	Saturday	Monday	Tuesday	Wedsday	Thursday	AMOUNT		OBSERVATIONS
— Foremen —										
W. Roy	Boilermaker							5	5	
I. Blackwood	do							3	10	
A. Frost	Fitter		from 3h to 30pl	upday	6 days			2	16 8	Went down until 1st February 1912
R. Adair	Erector							4	·	
I. Fox	do							4	·	
I. M'Dougall	Turner							4	·	
A. M'Kay	Machineman							3	10	
G. Kelly	Smith							4	·	
S. Steele	Patternmaker							3	10	
W. Smith	Brass Finisher							3	10	
I. Cotter	Iron Moulder							5	5	
W. Baxter	do							3	10	
H. O'Neill	Brass Moulder							3	15	
A. M'Diarmid	Coppersmith							4	5	Attached
							£	54	16 8 4	

Page from Harland and Wolff Wages Book, for the weeks ending 25 April and 2 May 1912.
Artie Frost's name is third from top for both weeks.

(Public Record Office, Belfast, D2805/W8/2/3)

14

A more uncertain way of gaining employment, especially for labourers, was the daily hiring session that took place at the area in the shipyard known as the Village Square. Here, each morning, the ritual was carried out as a foreman or journeyman picked his casual workers from the assembled crowd. This system was grossly unfair — if the foreman did not like the look of someone, the man would have little chance of work, and no work meant no pay.

For those in work, there was a unique form of timekeeping. In the time office were the timekeepers, who were each responsible for up to four hundred workers and their 'bourds'. These were small pieces of hard wood, approximately 1½ inches by 3 inches in size, with two small shoulders cut into the smaller side. In this space was stamped the workman's number. When a workman clocked in in the morning, his bourd was issued to him. He carried it all day, and if he needed special equipment during the day, the bourd would be given to the storeman as a deposit. If the equipment was not returned, the bourd was held, and this would have financial implications. At the end of the day the bourd was returned to the time office and the day's wages calculated. It was quite simple — no bourd, no pay.

There is a story that at quitting time, the exiting workers would not take the time to hand in their bourds individually, but would throw them *en masse* into the time office, to the cowering timekeepers. The small hatches in the time office windows might lead one to think that the story is unlikely, but perhaps the men had a 'true eye'.

Harland and Wolff Time Offices.

(Ulster Folk and Transport Museum. Photograph reproduced courtesy the Trustees of National Museums Northern Ireland)

In his book *Viscount Pirrie of Belfast*, Herbert Jefferson pays a glowing tribute to the workforce of the shipyard. He states:

> Directors and Managers are only one side of any firm's success: what of the tens of thousands of loyal, devoted, pride-taking workmen in the Belfast yard. These great men must not be overlooked. Take them away, and men at the top are helpless, and up may go the shutters. Fortunately these men, generations of them from early days, have been dependable and trustworthy. They have always been as keen as the very Directors for a finely finished and superb ship; the Belfast shipyard workers have been, and are still unsurpassed as the most competent and best trained shipbuilders and engineers in the world.[1]

15

On 31 July 1908, Harland and Wolff and the White Star Line agreed to the construction of two large vessels. Harland and Wolff described this process as 'contracting for'. The ships would indeed be large: each one would be over 880 feet long, with 46,328 gross tonnage. They would be triple-screw, with

engines capable of propelling them through the water at a speed of 21 knots. The second ship would be certified to carry 2,603 passengers. No names for the vessels were released at this stage, but shipyard numbers of 400 and 401 were issued to them.

16

A few weeks later, on 17 September, the directors gave orders to both the shipyard and the engine works to proceed with preparations for construction. Over the next weeks and months, various consultations and meetings took place between Harland and Wolff and the White Star Line. All of the heads of department in the shipyard would have been involved. In 1910, those positions were held by the following people:

Engine Works	Mr G. Cumming
Electrical	Mr W. Kempster
Designing	Mr T. Andrews
Contracts	Mr Gracey
Accounts	Mr Tawse[2]

(Directly under the chief designer, Thomas Andrews, worked a man named Edward Wilding. After the *Titanic* disaster, he would be called to the British Inquiry to give evidence on behalf of the shipyard. He also produced detailed calculations regarding the sinking. Following Andrews' death, Wilding was appointed head of the Designing Department. This appointment, after approval by the Board, meant that Wilding would have the privilege of lunching in the company's subsidiary dining room with the other heads of department.)

The Arroll Gantry under which Olympic *and* Titanic *would be built.*

(Ulster Folk and Transport Museum. Photograph reproduced courtesy the Trustees of National Museums Northern Ireland)

On 16 December 1908, at No. 2 slip, under the new Arroll Gantry, the keel of ship No. 400 — the *Olympic* — was laid. On 22 March 1909, at No. 3 slip, the keel for the second ship on order, No.401 — the *Titanic* — was laid.[3]

Hydraulic riveting of centre plate on Olympic.

(Ulster Folk and Transport Museum. Photograph reproduced courtesy the Trustees of National Museums Northern Ireland)

This date, 22 March, also saw two other notable maritime events in Belfast. Firstly, the Belfast Harbour Commissioners began work to deepen the Victoria Channel, to provide facilities for the movement of the new larger transatlantic steamers which were under construction. This action would increase the depth of the channel to 32 feet. Instead of using the material dredged up as landfill, the Commissioners decided to dump it near Blackhead, at the northern entrance to Belfast Lough. The work would take almost two and a half years to complete, and would cost in the region of £30,000. Secondly, a new transatlantic crossing record was set by the Cunard Line's *Mauretania*. She had sailed from New York to Queens-town in four days, eighteen hours and thirty-five minutes, at an average speed of 25.61 knots. The farthest she travelled in one day during this record-breaking crossing was 609 miles.

On 26 February 1909, orders were given to the shipyard and the engine works to proceed with the construction of the boilers of both ships. Construction of

18

the *Titanic* was behind that of the *Olympic*, but by 15 May 1909 she was framed (her steel ribbing was in place) to the height of the double bottom. On 20 April, orders were given to proceed with the construction and purchase of the rest of the machinery for the *Titanic*, and by 6 April 1910 she was fully framed. Six months later, on 19 October, the steel plates on her hull were all in place; and on 31 May 1911, with no naming ceremony, the *Titanic* was launched.

Everything about *SS 401* was gigantic. The steel plating that made up her hull was large and heavy; each plate measured 6 x 30 feet. The overlap of the plates was triple-riveted, with the riveting at the shelter deck and boat deck hydraulically riveted with new machinery purchased by the shipyard. The turn of the hull at the bilge keels, where the hull-side met the bottom, was also hydraulically riveted. The bilge keels were 25 inches deep and fitted for almost 300 feet of the length of the hull. The engine-room space for the reciprocating engines (large steam engines) was the largest of all the watertight compartments, about 60 feet long. The turbine room was 57 feet long, as were the boiler rooms.

The two reciprocating engines, which were made to Harland's long-tried design, would each turn one wing propeller shaft. They were designed as four-crank type, working at a pressure of 215 p.s.i. and exhausting the steam at about 9 p.s.i. This steam was directed to a Parsons-type steam turbine which would turn the central propeller shaft. The rotor on this turbine was 12 feet in diameter; its blades were between 18 and 25½ inches in length. The total length of the turbine was nearly 14 feet. This central turbine could, in an emergency, be turned by an electric motor.

Engine works at Harland & Wolff circa 1912.

(Ulster Folk and Transport Museum. Photograph reproduced courtesy the Trustees of National Museums Northern Ireland)

Lowering a boiler into Britannic *at outfitting wharf.*

(Ulster Folk and Transport Museum. Photograph reproduced courtesy the Trustees of National Museums Northern Ireland)

Two anchors were delivered by Harkness, a local haulier. A team of twenty horses was needed to pull each of the 15½-ton anchors; each link in the anchor chain weighed 175 pounds. The man in charge of delivering this load would later make another long and heavy journey — to Ardara House in Comber, to bring the telegram telling the Andrews family that their son Thomas had been lost with the *Titanic*.

The steering gear at the stern was fitted on the shelter deck. It was also huge: the diameter of the rudder stock was almost 24 inches. The gear followed Harland's wheel-and-pinion design, working through a spring quadrant on the rudder head. Two independent engines to move the rudder were installed on either side of it. Either engine could move the rudder on its own; the other acted as an emergency back-up. This gear was controlled from the main bridge by telemotors, and from the docking bridge by mechanical means.

The stern frame which was to hold the three propellers and their shafts was made by the Darlington Forge Company and arrived in Belfast from Darlington in December 1909. It weighed around 190 tons. The shafts to the propellers were slightly over 20 inches in diameter. The propellers themselves were made from manganese bronze; each one had four blades and was about 16½ feet in diameter.

To assist navigation, four compasses were fitted: two on the bridge, one on the aft docking bridge, and one on a brass platform in the centre of the ship, 12 feet above the ironwork and 78 feet above the water-line.

The *Titanic* was rigged as a two-masted vessel, and these masts would also support the aerial wires for the Marconi wireless. The aerial had to be high enough that the gases emitted by the funnels would not interfere with it; because of this, the aerial was 30 feet above the top of the funnels, with the masts at a height of 205 feet above the water-line.

To generate electricity, four 400-kilowatt engines and dynamos were fitted; they had a power rating of 580 horsepower, running at about 325 revolutions per minute. The total output from the dynamos was about 16,000 amperes at 100 volts. Two emergency dynamos were also provided.

Electric lifts for the *Titanic* were supplied by Messrs R. Waygood; they were installed and working by February 1910.

The cost to the White Star Line for this new liner would be in the region of £1,500,000.

* * *

Many of the shipyard's old workers have stories about what the yard was like at the time when the *Titanic* was being built. Over 3 million rivets would be used to hold the *Titanic*'s plates together to make her watertight. The shipyard's riveting squads were revered by the rest of the workforce. Gordon Roberts — who, in his time, worked for Harland and Wolff — remembers these squads well. He explained that there were five people in each squad: the heater-boy, the catch-boy, the holder-on, and the two riveters.

> The heater-boy was responsible for the furnace, which was fuelled by coke. There was a blower system, which the heater-boy would operate with his foot, to force air over the coke. One of the heater-boy's responsibilities was to ensure that the furnace was ready to go first thing on Monday morning after the weekend break. Many a young heater-boy would be well prepared. Stories are told of these boys breaking in to the shipyard on Sunday evenings and setting the fire so that, when the horn sounded in the morning, the fire would be lit and the first rivet of the day would be heated as quickly as possible.
>
> The heater-boy was trained to watch the rivet heating up; when it reached a certain colour, he would lift it out of the furnace with a pair of tongs. A steel plate was laid between the furnace and the area of riveting. The heater-boy would slide the rivet along the steel plating, where it would be caught by the catch-boy's tongs.

The catch-boy would then run as quickly as he could to the area where the riveters were working and pass the hot rivet to the holder-on.

The holder-on's job was to put the rivet in the hole in the two overlapping plates, and to hold it in place while the riveters shaped the head from the other side of the plates. There were two riveters, one right-handed and one left-handed. Once the rivet appeared in the hole, both riveters would set to work, in perfect harmony. The sound from a good pair of riveters would echo across the yard as a clear, rhythmic thump-thump.

On payday, the squad was paid collectively for the number of rivets worked that week. They would normally make their way to the pub, where the payment was split between the five of them. With the two riveters receiving more money than the other members of the squad. [4]

Tradesmen called 'caulkers' dressed the gaps between the riveted steel plates and pumped key joints with putty forced in by a hydraulic pump. Bill McClean, who was an apprentice caulker in 1909, told the following story of life in the shipyard.

When asked, 'How do you know if the hull is watertight before the launch?' He would answer, 'If she'll keep water in, she'll keep water out!' He continued:

> As the work progresses, each section of the ship is flooded with water and the outside checked for leaks. In order that the flooded area may be emptied easily, a drain hole is drilled in the lowest part of the area. The hole is tapped, then plugged with a suitable bolt. To remove the water after testing, the bolt is partially unscrewed, a piece of string is wound on, and — standing well clear — the men pull the string to unwind the bolt and allow the water to drain. Some of the sections were so large that they would take days to empty.[5]

Bill told his son William the story of how he was given a ratchet drill and told to drill a hole in the bottom plating of a section of hull. He was shown how to set the equipment up and left to get on with it. After ratcheting for two days, he had made no impression on the metal — although he had succeeded in polishing up the area to be drilled! Young Bill was almost in tears when an 'old lag' — an experienced worker — took him to the side and showed him how to sharpen the drill bit with a file. Bob returned to the drilling site, and within minutes he had cut the hole.

Another interesting account of life in the shipyard in this period comes from joiner Hugh McRoberts, who was born in 1891. His son-in-law, Brian Millar, remembers Hugh telling him about an incident with a colleague.

> My father-in-law was a joiner who worked on the grand staircase of the *Titanic*. Most of the work was carried out in the joiners' shop, and the finished components were taken onto the ship and fitted in position. A colleague of Hugh's was hand-carving a piece of hardwood to go on the base of one of the staircase newel posts. When the piece was completed, he took it to the ship to fit it; but he returned to the joiners' shop shortly afterwards, in a very worried state, and told my father-in-law that the trim had split as he fitted it to the newel post.

In those days, if any material was damaged, the cost of the wasted material was deducted from the employee's wages, so the joiner had every reason to be worried.

Hugh told me that the two of them had a think about what to do and decided to make up a mixture of glue and sawdust and pack the split; they hoped that, after polishing, the join would not be noticed. So, without a word to anyone, the two set about the deed; and they got away with it.

There is a sequel to this story. Shortly after the ship sank, this workman came over to Hugh and whispered to him, 'They'll never find the fault now.' My father-in-law said it was spoken in all seriousness and with a feeling of great relief. There is no question but that the man was as conscious as all the others of the enormity of the tragedy, but I suppose he had his own priorities, and a full wage packet was one of them.[6]

* * *

No.	Name	Launched	Delivered	Owners
396	Memphian	23. Jan. '08	20th Feb '08	Fredk Leyland &Co
397	Minnewaska	12. Nov. '08	24th April '09	Atlantic Transpt Co
398	Mercian	16. Apl. '08	16th May '08	Wilsons & Furness-Leyland
399	Megantic	10 Dec '08	3. June '09	White Star Line
400	Olympic	20th Octr. 1910	29th May 1911	Do
401	Titanic	31st May 1911	2nd April 1912	Do
402	Leopoldville (Anvers)	13. Aug. '08	10 Nov. '08	Compagnie Belge Maritime du Congo
403	Leicestershire	3. June '09	11 Sep '09	Bibby Steamship Co
404	Karoola (Melbourne)	9 Mar. '09	8 July 1909	McIlwraith, McEacharn & Co
405	Pierbice (Belfast)	6. May '09	8 July 1909	Royal Mail Steam Packet
406	Balantia (do)	28 Oct. '09	18th Decr. 1909	Do
	Suevic (new bow)	5th October '07		
407	Mallina (Brisbane)	25. March '09	29. April '09	Aust. Galician U.S.N.Co
408	Meltonian	8 July '09	17th August, 1909	Wilson & Furness-Leyland Line
409	Pakeha (Southampton)	26th May, 1910	20th August, 1910	Shaw Savill & Albion Co
410	Edinburgh Castle (London)	27th January 1910	28th April, 1910	Union-Castle Co
411	Gloucestershire	8th July, 1910	22nd Octr. 1910	Bibby Steam Ship Co
K	Neptune	Machinery only 30th Nov. 1910		Admiralty
412	Themistocles	22nd Sept 1910	12th Jan. 1911	Geo Thompson & Co Ltd
413	Baden Württemberg 'Sachsen'	14th Novr. 1910	21st Jan 1911	Hamburg-American Line
414	Maloja	17th Decr 1910	7th Sept 1911	P & O Co.

Attention to detail was meticulous. Inspectors from the Board of Trade made frequent trips to examine the progress of the work, checking everything down to the 3-inch camber that was built into the *Titanic*'s deck. Health and safety standards for the workforce, however — and this is no reflection on the shipyard today — were not up to those set, eighty-five years later, by the implementation of current health and safety laws. Accidents and deaths occurred on a regular basis. For example, on SS 412, the *Themistocles*, Richard Higgins, a plater from East Belfast, died after a fall of 24 feet; SS 427, the *Darro*, saw an Englishman from Newcastle-upon-Tyne, John Gordon, die from a fractured skull after a fall of 40 feet.

During the construction of the *Olympic* and the *Titanic*, over 450 men were hurt and seventeen died.

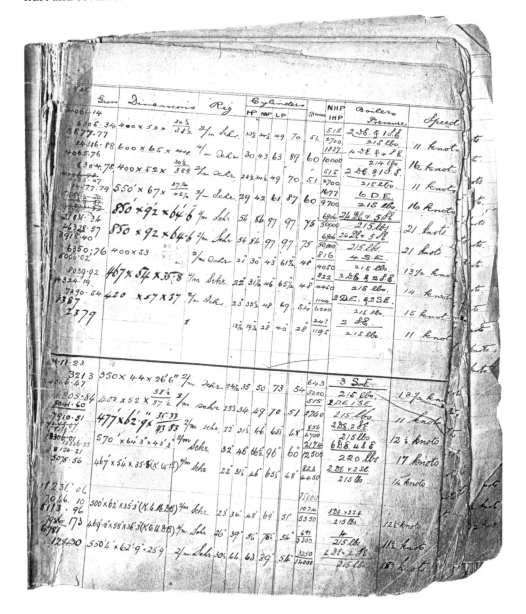

Ships' Details
(Public Record Office, Belfast, D2805/Ship/3)

24

N° 407 Triple SS. Titanic   O.S.N Co.

1908

July 31 Contracted for
Sep 17 S.Y & E.W. ordered to proceed, except with machinery
Mar 22 Keel laid — N° 3 ship
Feb. 26 S.Y. & E.W. ordered to proceed with boilers
May 15 Framed to height of D.B.
Apr 20 S.Y. & E.W. ordered to proceed with remainder of machinery
Apr 6 Fully framed
Oct 19 Plated
May 31 Launched
Apr 2 Delivered

Exact dates for Titanic's *progress.*

(Public Record Office, Belfast, D2805/Ship/1)

On 10 April 1912, a report detailing the deaths and accidents which had occurred during the construction and fitting-out of the *Titanic* was made to the normal managers' meeting at the shipyard. The final figures listed eight fatal, twenty-eight severe and 218 slight accidents.

The records show that of the eight fatal accidents on the *Titanic*, six were in the shipyard and two in the works. Following detailed research I have been able to positively identify five of the eight men who died whilst working on the *Titanic*. Should not their names be remembered along with those of the many who were to perish when the ship sank?

On 20 April 1910, Samuel J. Scott, a catch-boy, aged fifteen, from Templemore Street, Belfast, died from a fractured skull after he fell from a ladder on the staging.

On 23 June 1910, John Kelly, a heater-boy, aged nineteen, from Convention Street, Belfast, died from shock after falling from the slipway onto the ground.

On 5 November 1910, William Clarke, a driller, aged twenty-seven, from Coulter Street, Belfast, fell from staging; he died two days later, on 7 November.

On 31 May 1911, James Dobbin, a shipwright from Merret Street, Belfast, was injured during the launch of the *Titanic* when he was crushed under falling timber; he died on 1 June.

On 13 June 1911, Robert James Murphy, a rivet-counter from Hillman Street, Belfast, died from a fractured skull after the staging he was standing on collapsed and he fell 30 feet. His son, Robert Murphy Junior, died during the construction of the *Olympic*.

9

Nº 401 – ss. "Titanic"

Further to our memo. of the 8th June last, giving particulars of the number and cost of accidents on the ss. "Olympic"; the following is a summary of the accidents which occurred in connection with the "Titanic" and of the compensation paid in respect thereof.

	Shipyard						Engine Works					
	Fatal	Cost	Severe	Cost	Slight	Cost	Fatal	Cost	Severe	Cost	Slight	Cost
On ships (during construction and fitting out)	6	£795.5.2	18	759.2.8	99	420.3.3	–	—	2	90.8.0	35	102.6.6
In Works (shops sheds &c)	2	338.13.0	4	342.13.7	56	234.11.8	–	—	4	662.9.0	28	93.10.7
Total	8	£1133.18.2	22	2101.16.3	155	664.14.11	–	—	6	752.17.0	63	195.17.1

	Shipyard	Engine Works	Grand Total
Accidents	185	69	254
Cost	£3900.9.4	£948.14.1	£4.849.3.5

The figures include all compensation paid up to the date of the vessel's departure, 2nd April 1912, together with an estimate of the amounts required to meet the claims still outstanding at that date. After these have been disposed of, a final and complete return will be furnished.

(Intld) W.T.   (Intld) J.F.R.

Date 10th April 1912.

Director's minute book, detailing accidents during construction.

(Public Record Office, Belfast, D2805/MIN/A/2)

A similar report on the *Olympic* was submitted to the managers' meeting on 8 June 1911. This report stated that nine fatal, fourteen severe and 206 slight accidents had occurred during work on her. One man, Joseph Sharpe, was even shot by a workmate while working on the *Olympic*; fortunately, Mr Sharpe survived.

Some of those who died while working on the *Olympic* were:

- John Bell, who died on 15 October 1909, after falling from staging.
- George Simpson, a heater-boy, who died on 22 November 1909.
- Robert Murphy Jr, who fell 60 feet and was killed on 6 December 1910.
- His father was to die later during construction of the *Titanic*.

During the period between 1909 and 1912, other men died in the shipyard, including:

- John Moffat, a painter, who died on 7 June 1910 from a fractured skull after being hit by a travelling crane.
- Adam E. Smith, who died on 21 June 1910 after being crushed by an iron plate.
- Samuel Haire (a relative of the author's wife), a shipwright, who died on 28 September 1910 after a plank of wood fell over 80 feet on him.
- William Flanagan, a stager, who died on 2 December 1910 after being hit by a falling piece of timber.

I have discovered three other fatal accidents at the relevant time:

- Robert Bell, a plater's helper from Armagh, living at Lyons Street, Belfast, was crushed under iron plates and died on 22 August 1910.
- Ernest Morgan, a painter from Roxborough Street, Belfast, died on 12 February 1912 from a fractured skull after being hit by a travelling crane.
- Stephen M. Gracey, a thirty-year-old labourer from Glenalpin Street, Belfast, died on 21 March 1912 from a fractured pelvis and ruptured spleen after being crushed by a casting in the moulding shop.

* * *

Over the years, there has been much controversy over who was actually responsible for the design of the three Olympic-class liners, the *Olympic*, the *Titanic* and the *Britannic*.

In the years before these liners were built, the White Star Line had slipped behind their rivals the Cunard shipping company. In 1906 Cunard had launched the *Lusitania* and the *Mauretania*; the size, elegance and speed of these ships had shaken the world. Joseph Bruce Ismay, the chairman of the White Star Line, could see his company losing out badly to Cunard in the battle to control shipping on the prestigious North Atlantic route.

Ismay formed an alliance with William Pirrie, the chairman of Harland and Wolff — Harland and Wolff agreed not to build ships for White Star's competitors, and White Star agreed to place all their orders at the Belfast yard. In 1907, during an after-dinner discussion in Pirrie's London home, Downshire House, Ismay and Pirrie came up with the first seeds of the idea for the Olympic-class liners.

The chairman of the White Star Line, Joseph Bruce Ismay, and his wife, Florence, on a staircase on board the Teutonic.

(Ulster Folk and Transport Museum. Photograph reproduced courtesy the Trustees of National Museums Northern Ireland)

Pirrie would have brought the simple sketches that they drew up that night back to Belfast. But who transformed their ideas from a simple sketch into the largest vessels that the world of 1912 had ever seen?

The answer, I believe, lies in an article printed after the disaster.

The Rt. Hon. Alexander M. Carlisle
'The Man who built the R.M.S. *Titanic* ?'

In an interview in London with Mrs Cecil Chesterton (sister-in-law of G.K. Chesterton) which appeared in her family-owned periodical, Mr Alexander Carlisle, after he retired as Chairman and Managing Director of Harland and Wolff in 1910, claimed: 'I was responsible for the designing and building of some of our greatest ships, from the *Oceanic*, the first of the White Star Line, 3,807 gross tons, down to the *Titanic*, on which one of my dearest friends, W. Stead, was drowned.'

Later in the interview, Carlisle stated that he was at Southampton docks, to see Stead off to America, when the *Titanic* set out on her ill-fated maiden voyage.

Stead was a dear friend of mine, and to the last day of my life I shall regret that I was not with him on the *Titanic*.... It was just a toss-up that I wasn't on board. I'd gone down to see her sail, and just before she was off Bruce Ismay [Chairman of the White Star Line] shouted out to me (standing on the quayside), 'Why don't you come with us, Carlisle?' I replied, 'I have not been asked.'

Chesterton asked Carlisle whether, if Ismay had asked him to come, he would have gone aboard. Carlisle replied, 'I would have.'

Regarding his career at Harland and Wolff's shipyard — where his cousin and brother-in-law Lord Pirrie (who was married to Carlisle's sister) was a member and later Chairman of the firm — Carlisle told Mrs Chesterton:

I went to work as a boy of sixteen. I was apprenticed as a shipbuilder to Harland and Wolff and remained there for forty years. In those early days we worked a week of sixty hours, beginning at six in the morning, and I dare say I felt tired occasionally. But I was a strong and healthy lad — indeed, I have never known what it was to be really ill throughout my life — and I had the best mother in the world. She was the finest woman I have ever known.

For amusement, I never went in for sport; my two hobbies have always remained the same — biking and cold-water bathing. I always have my morning tub, and never a day passes but I go bicycling somewhere in the park or through the City (London), past the Bank. The denser the traffic, the more fun I get. I never believed in coddling, and have no use for an overcoat, however cold the day may be.

I worked through all the shops at Harland and Wolff's, learning each branch of the trade, and at the finish was manager of the whole business. Yes, I was responsible for designing and building some of our greatest ships. I can tell you about some of the big ships.... I can tell you we felt proud when we finished the *Olympic* in 1910. You must remember that in those days the world wasn't used to vessels of her size; in fact, she represented a big step forward in marine architecture, perhaps the biggest the world has ever seen.

In 1889 we launched the *Teutonic* and the *Majestic*, successors to the *Oceanic*. They appeared at the Jubilee review [by Queen Victoria and the young Kaiser-elect] at Spithead as armed cruisers of 9,984 gross tons, an advance of nearly 5,000 tons on the *Germanic* and the *Britannic* — two of the finest ships we ever built — in 1874. The *Olympic*, with 45,000 gross tonnage, topped the lot. Then, in 1912, came the *Titanic* and her sister ship the *Britannic*.

Did I ever think, as a boy apprentice, that I would run the show? Well, we all have our dreams, though I was mostly concerned to get through my work and home to my mother [who was a Montgomery from the region of Aldergrove, near the shores of Lough Neagh].

Alexander Carlisle
(Illustrated London News)

Carlisle was Chief Naval Architect of the shipyard for many years. In 1910, he retired as head of the shipyard and moved from Belfast to London, where he later gave evidence to the *Titanic* Inquiry on his plans for the liner and the number of lifeboats he had in his plans. When Carlisle retired, he was succeeded by his cousin, Thomas Andrews Jr, who completed the work on the *Titanic* — the original designs for the *Olympic* and the *Titanic* were Carlisle's.

Alexander Montgomery Carlisle was the son of John Carlisle and Catherine Montgomery. Alexander came from a large family; his sister Margaret was to marry William James Pirrie in 1879. He was born in 1854 and joined Harland and Wolff as a premium apprentice in 1870, at the age of sixteen. His parents would have paid the shipyard a premium — normally one hundred guineas — for young Alexander to learn a trade. By all accounts, he worked hard and progressed through the various departments of the shipyard. By 1878 he had proven himself to be both a skilled shipbuilder and a book-keeper. By 1890 he had progressed to General Manager of the shipyard. On 7 March 1907, he had risen to the position of Chairman of the Managing Directors of Harland and Wolff.

In June 1910, Alexander Carlisle resigned from his position in the shipyard. His reasons for doing so have never been made public. Moss and Hume, in their book *Shipbuilders to the World*, suggest that he may have disliked the dictatorial ways of his brother-in-law, Lord Pirrie.

Was Carlisle the man responsible for the designing and building of the *Titanic*? When Pirrie met with Ismay and discussed the building of the Olympic-class liners, Pirrie, on his return to Belfast, would have summoned the Chief Naval Designer — Carlisle — and given him the brief for these new vessels. These instructions would have been passed down to the Drawing Office, and the various people there, including Thomas Andrews, Roderick Chisholm, and W.J. Smith (the assistant chief draughtsman), who, along with the other draughtsmen,

TITANIC – BELFAST'S OWN

would have produced the various plans. In the interview with Mrs Chesterton, Carlisle boasts that he '... was responsible for the designing and building of our greatest ships, up to and including the *Titanic*.'

After the *Titanic* sank, Carlisle was called to the British Inquiry held by Lord Mersey. He gave his evidence on Monday 10 June 1912, the twentieth day of the Inquiry. Under examination by Mr Butler Aspinall KC, who represented the Board of Trade, Carlisle was asked whether he '... took part in working out the designs of the *Olympic* and the *Titanic*'. He replied: 'Yes. They were entirely designed practically by Lord Pirrie. The details, the decorations, the equipments and general arrangements all came under me.'[7]

In the early years of the century, Pirrie was taking full control of the shipyard, and he needed directors who would not question his ideas too deeply. Among his group of managing directors were J.W. Kempster, Thomas Andrews and George Cumming; all of these men had been promoted to their current positions by Pirrie. Such was the degree of control that Pirrie wished to have over his managing directors, that it was he who went seeking orders to build ships and then gave the orders to proceed with these plans. He also took responsibility for the measurements and engines of the ships; he even went as far as deciding which slip each ship should be built on.

Carlisle was also a member of this committee of directors; he, however, had not been put in place by Pirrie. Carlisle was an outspoken man, and would certainly have questioned Pirrie. Another action of Carlisle's might have increased the discontent between him and Pirrie: in 1906, Carlisle decided to stand for the Parliamentary elections in West Belfast, as an Independent candidate. This split the Unionist vote, and the Nationalist candidate, Joseph Devlin, won the seat by a margin of sixteen votes. Pirrie, a possible Unionist candidate for the seat, would not have been pleased. It is also worth remembering that Carlisle's proposal for the number of lifeboats on the *Titanic* was drastically reduced by the White Star Line.

With all this in mind, it is easy to imagine that Carlisle might have felt somewhat sidelined by Pirrie; and it is not surprising that he decided to have his day with the press.

The fact is that Pirrie controlled the Harland and Wolff shipyard, and that the designs of the *Olympic* and the *Titanic* were his. But it was Carlisle who carried out the instructions and orders given by his brother-in-law, and who brought Ismay and Pirrie's vision to life.

CHAPTER 3

The Thompson Graving Dock

With amazing foresight, the Belfast Harbour Commissioners decided — in late 1902, four years before the new Olympic-class liners were even imagined — to build a new dry dock in Belfast. This new dock was to be over 80 feet longer than their then-largest facility of this kind, the Alexandra dock.

Did the forward-looking Commissioners have even the slightest idea what Lord Pirrie, J. Bruce Ismay, Harland and Wolff and the White Star Line were up to? Or were the new Olympic-class liners actually planned before 1906 — the date when, during after-dinner discussions between Ismay and Pirrie at Pirrie's London home, these new liners were supposedly first planned?

A clue to the answers to these questions can be found in a speech which Lord Pirrie made in September 1922, in Glasgow, at the Annual Dinner of the Clyde Trust. Pirrie, who had become a member of the Belfast Harbour Commissioners in 1893, said of the co-operation between the Harbour Commissioners and Harland and Wolff:

> We have never built a ship that the Harbour Commissioners of Belfast had not built a graving dock ready to accommodate that vessel the day we launched her.[1]

Was Pirrie involved in a bit of 'insider trading', or was he just looking after his and Harland and Wolff's best interests? In his speech he said that Belfast had taken the lead in building big ships because the dry-dock space was available. He also disagreed with the suggestion that dry docks, or graving docks, did not pay because they provided no visible return; he asked whether roads, for example, offered any visible profits. Graving docks, he concluded, were absolutely necessary if Harland and Wolff were to carry out fully their mission of shipbuilding.

The plan to construct the Thompson graving dock was decided upon in 1902, and the contract was drawn up in 1903. Construction work was to commence in 1904.

The main contractors were Messrs Walter Scott and Middleton of Westminster. The chief engineer was Mr W. Redfern Kelly, JP, M.Inst. CE, and the resident engineer was Mr T.S. Gilbert, M.Inst. CE. Other contractors involved were the Belfast firms of McLaughlin and Harvey, who were responsible for the pumping station, and W.J. Campbell, who laid the brickwork and reinforced concrete.

The total cost of the seven-year contract was in the region of £350,000. Up to five hundred men were employed in the construction. Some idea of the sheer size of the dock can be given by the amount of material excavated: over 300,000 cubic yards of sand and clay were removed, and 76,000 cubic yards of concrete, 24,000 cubic yards of brickwork and 36,000 cubic feet of granite stonework were built into the structure.

It was originally envisaged that the work would take about three and a half years, but as a result of unforeseen circumstances, this period of time was nearly doubled. One of the main reasons for the delay was the subsidence of the adjacent Alexandra dry dock, which collapsed on 4 October 1905 because of the excavation work on the Thompson dock. The Alexandra dock had to be closed for nearly two years to allow for repairs, which increased the time taken to complete the Thompson dock.

The Alexandra dock, which had been designed in 1885, was at the time the biggest dry dock in Belfast, but at 800 feet long it could not accommodate any major increase in the size of shipping. The new Thompson dock would, however, be able to accommodate ships up to 887 feet 6 inches long. A detailed look at the dimensions gives us some idea of the enormous size of this structure:

Width at coping level	128 feet
Depth of floor below high tide level	32 feet 9 inches
Thickness of floor at centre	17 feet 6 inches
Thickness of walls at base	18 feet 9 inches
Volume of water when full	approximately 23 million gallons

When the project was first considered, plans were submitted for three sizes of dock — the first, 750 feet in length, the second, 800 feet, and the third, 850 feet. Eventually it was decided to build the largest. (The length of the dock could be increased by another 37½ feet by placing the caisson — the water-tight gate arrangement — on the outer face of the dock gate.) It was fortunate that the Commissioners decided on this size, or there would not have been a dry dock large enough to accommodate the new super-ships.

Three 1,000-horsepower pumping engines were installed to pump the water out of the dock. An extra-powerful pump was provided as a leakage engine for removing drainage water, and four boilers were provided to power the pumps. The three pumps could drain the full dock in about a hundred minutes; normally, however, only two pumps would work together, with the third acting as an emergency standby.

Two capstans with a 30-ton capacity and three with an 11-ton capacity were provided. In 1911, no other dry dock in the world had such large-capacity capstans; even those in Admiralty yards would normally only be rated at about 16 tons. The capstans, along with the caisson and the water inlet sluices, were worked by hydraulic power generated by two 155-horsepower engines with a working pressure of 750 p.s.i. or 51 bar.

The entrance to the dock was closed by means of a large rectangular steel structure, called a caisson, which was carried on two lines of heavy rollers. The whole structure could be moved to seal on the inside or the outside granite face of the dock; with the caisson housed on the outside, the length of the dock was increased by 37½ feet.

On the floor of the dock were laid 332 massive keel-blocks of cast iron with timber capping-pieces. A ship would rest on these blocks while being completed.

The Harbour Commissioners also had a new, large, outfitting wharf constructed close to the graving dock. To give access to the dock, Queen's Road was extended by over 300 feet, and a new road 1,150 feet in length was laid. A tramway, which could accommodate rolling loads of up to 150 tons, was also laid. The Commissioners also had the channel at West Twin Island widened to allow the proposed new ships to manoeuvre, so that they would not have to turn in Belfast Lough. This work cost in the region of £9,400. The river opposite the new fitting-out wharf and the approaches to the graving dock were dredged to a depth of 32 feet.

Construction of Thompson Dock.

(Ulster Museum Belfast.
Photograph reproduced courtesy
the Trustees of National
Museums Northern Ireland)

34

Steam crane dating from 1912, used at Thompson Dry Dock.

(Author's collection)

The Official Opening of the Thompson Dock

The official opening of the dock took place on the morning of Saturday, 1 April 1911. The first ship into the dock was the White Star Line's *Olympic*, to undergo fitting-out and work on her hull.

During the previous night — the night of 31 March — water had been allowed to enter the dock slowly. By 10.30, on the morning of 1 April, a large crowd had gathered at the dockside. This group had been specially invited — admittance was by ticket only. Those who arrived without a ticket had to make do with a view from some distance away.

The Harbour Commissioners had travelled from Donegall Quay on the *SS Musgrave*, leaving the quay at about 10.15 a.m. The Chairman of the Board — Robert Thompson MP, DL, after whom the new dock was to be named — had with him some distinguished guests, including the Right Honourable Lord Justice Cherry, the Honourable Mr Justice Boyd, Mr Crawford McCullagh, High Sheriff of Belfast, Sir William Ewart, Mr John Gordon KC, MP, Mr James Chambers KC MP and Mr W. McGrath KC.

The *SS Musgrave* was berthed at the Alexandra wharf, and the guests went ashore for a better view. Lord Pirrie, accompanied by Lady Pirrie, was directing events. Thomas Andrews was also present, with Mr John Dickson, Head Manager of Harland and Wolff.

Above: Olympic *fully in dock.*

(Both — Ulster Folk and Transport Museum.
Photographs reproduced courtesy the Trustees
of National Museums Northern Ireland)

The Olympic *was the first ship into the dock*
after the official opening.

At around 10.00 a.m., scores of workmen, with two tugs, the *Hercules* and the *Jackal*, began to move the *Olympic* into the dock. Communication between the tugs and the *Olympic* was by megaphone and a coded system of whistle-blows. The bow of the *Olympic* crossed the line into the new dock, with only 3½ feet to spare at the entrance gates, at about 10.50 a.m., and by 11.35 a.m., the *Olympic* was safely and completely installed in the dock.

Before the *Olympic* had been towed to the dock, two divers had inspected her hull to ensure that no wooden stays from her launch were still attached. These stays could have snagged against the gates as the ship entered the dock and caused serious problems.

The workmen then began to pump the dock out. This work was undertaken slowly, in stages, to allow the *Olympic* to settle, and also to allow side-props to be fitted between her hull and the wall of the dock, in order to stop her moving from side to side. This took until about 6.30 p.m. and finally, by about 9.00 p.m., all of the water had been pumped out of the dock.

After the *Olympic* had been docked, luncheon was served on board the *SS Majestic* for the invited guests. Mr Robert Thompson proposed the toast: 'Success to the *Olympic*'.[2] Lord Pirrie said in his speech that not only the Harbour Commissioners, but also the citizens of Belfast, should feel gratified at the completion of the new dock.

The dock and pump house has ceased to be used and now are under the auspices of the Northern Ireland Science Park. The gate has been sealed and a new railing and information boards have been placed around the edge of the dock. The pump house has been turned into a tourist attraction.

Thompson Dry Dock today.

(Author's collection)

CHAPTER 4

A Gentle Shove

Walter Lord, in his book *The Night Lives On*, quotes a shipyard worker as explaining to a visitor at the launch of the *Titanic*: 'They just builds 'er and shoves 'er in.'[1] And in 1912 — especially as there was no naming ceremony — it must have seemed to those gathered to watch a launch that, indeed, Harland and Wolff just shoved 'er in.

Nothing could be further from the truth. The fact that the launches went so smoothly was a compliment to the organisation within the shipyard. The process of launching a ship was a very complicated manoeuvre, requiring prior planning and meticulous attention to detail for several months before the launch date.

A few days before the launch, a slipway — a timber platform, running up to the ship and under the keel, down which the ship would slide into the water — was constructed. When the ship was being built, a space was left under the keel to allow this slipway to be fitted and secured. Tons of tallow (the best type for a launching was cows' tallow) were boiled to make a launching grease. Oil was then added to the boiling vat of fat, to reduce the risk of the tallow freezing, and either sperm oil or castor oil was added, in a proportion of about five percent of the weight of the tallow. This mixture was then spread on the slipway to a depth of about a quarter of an inch.

Prior to 1898, when a ship was launched, it was held in place by heavy wooden props under the keel. When the signal was given to send the vessel down the slipway, workmen under the hull would dislodge these props with a large metal sledge, several men pulling and several pushing. On occasion, this method failed to knock away the props. At such times, a workman had to go under the hull carrying a wooden pole with a large metal spike fixed to the top; he would hold this against the prop, above head-height, while other workmen with sledgehammers stood behind him and drove the spike into the prop in order to split it and release the ship. This method was extremely dangerous; if the sledgehammers missed their mark, the man holding the spiked pole ended up with a very sore head.

On 15 December 1898, Thomas Andrews noted in his diary that *SS No. 323*, the *Medic*, had been launched at 11.15 a.m., by a new system which used hydraulic triggers. Two triggers were set in place, one at each side of the ship, usually about halfway along the hull. The triggers did not push the ship down the slipway; rather, they held the ship in place by hydraulic pressure. When the order to launch the ship was given, both triggers were released by the throw of a lever, allowing the ship to slide into the water. There are stories of the triggers failing and launching the ship before the ceremony, but on the whole, the new launching system was far safer than the old one.

38

Right: Entry from Thomas Andrews' diary of 15 December 1898: 'SS No. 323 launched from No. 1 Slip at 11.15 a.m. with new hyd. tricker [sic] gear'.
(Andrews Collection)

Below: Bow cradle launching device.
(Ulster Folk and Transport Museum. Photograph reproduced courtesy the Trustees of National Museums Northern Ireland)

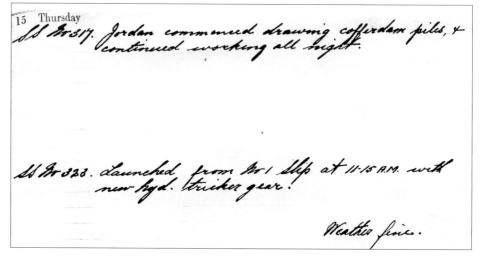

While the slipway was being prepared, other preparations for the launch were also under way. The owners of the vessel were written to, about ten days before the launch, and informed of the proposed date and time of the proceedings. They were asked to specify whether any guests would be crossing to Belfast. Stands were prepared for these invited guests. Various local groups, including the Belfast Harbour Commissioners, the Board of Trade, Lloyds of London, the Belfast harbour-master and the local police superintendent, were also informed of the proceedings.

Soundings were taken in the channel, at the bottom of the slip, and if needed the area would be dredged; there would be nothing more embarrassing than to send the vessel down the slip only to see her run aground because the channel was not deep enough.

An internal memo was sent to the engine works, asking if the engines and boilers would be ready to go on board after the launch and what cranes would be needed to lift them.

On the vessel, all the tanks were tested, and the men checked that all plates on the hull were closed, that all drain holes were filled and that all bulkheads were watertight. They also ensured that all the launching check-chains and wire ropes were in place; again, it would have been embarrassing if, after being launched, the vessel simply kept moving rather than coming to a halt in the water.

As the date of the launch approached, further preparations were made:

- If required, arrangements were made to have coal and water provided for the donkey boilers and to have men ready to attend to them, checking that they were lashed down.
- Any buoys in the water in the line of the launch were removed.
- Mooring-ropes were provided.
- A flagpole was placed at the stern of the vessel, and flags were supplied and placed on board.
- Ladders and fenders were placed on the vessel's side.
- The derricks and any ropes were cleared away from the launch area.
- The boom at the end of the slip was hauled away.
- A fitter ensured that the ballast-tank manholes were closed.
- A carpenter was required to be at the slip about an hour before the launch, to check that the anchors and chains were in order and to be ready for any cutting-away that was required.
- A caulker was ready to inspect the peaks and holds after the launch, to ensure that they were dry.
- Two flagboats, the tugs, and men who would be required to move the vessel

to the fitting-out wharf after the launch, were to be in place.

- In the event that the launch had to be assisted by steam, the apparatus was ordered and set in place, and the correct pressure was built up, prior to the ceremony.

- A large notice was placed adjacent to the hull of the vessel, stopping men from working on board.

- A wire was to be sent to the owners after the event, advising them that the vessel had been safely launched.

- A few days before the launch, the foremen and the captain of the tug met to discuss any last-minute problems.[2]

The final checks would have been completed long before Lord Pirrie and the other directors arrived. Pirrie would give everything a final inspection. This firm of his was the greatest shipbuilding yard in Britain, and it was important to Pirrie and to Harland and Wolff that all should go well at the launch. That was why the long and detailed checks were made — so that Pirrie could make the launching ceremony look easy. It had to look as if they had just shoved 'er in; and, with the shipyard's dedication and sheer professionalism, it did.

After the Launch

Just as there was a lengthy checklist to be gone through before a vessel was launched, so too there was a comprehensive checklist to be completed before a ship departed from the works at Queen's Island to her new owners. This included a check on the freeboard and a final check on the tonnage; the passenger certificate was inspected, and all tanks were filled. Tests were also run on the following:

Weather decks	Electric lights
Tunnels	Electric heaters
Derricks	Electric searchlights
Cargo cranes	Masthead lights
Steering gear and winches	Side lights
Steam fans	Fresh water system
Watertight doors	Refrigeration system
Fire extinguishers	Sanitary system
Galley ranges	Ballast system
Telephone systems	Steam heaters and winches[3]

The shipyard also ensured that ropes, flags, charts, compasses and parallel rulers for the bridge were on board. The office staff sent orders to the various departments in the shipyard to ensure that the following preparations were made for departure day:

- Steam was provided for the winches

- Tugs were provided to assist the ship's passage down the Lough
- Compasses were adjusted
- A request was made for a boat and pilot for the tow-ropes
- The crew that would man the vessel was assembled
- Riggers and labourers were assembled to see the vessel safely down the Lough
- Provisions for the vessel were ordered
- Meals for the departing crew were arranged; they would be supplied by the shipyard's dining-room
- A telegram was to be sent to Lord Pirrie, informing him when the vessel was safely down the Lough and when it reached its destination
- The owners were notified of the time of departure.[4]

When this lengthy process had been completed and the new vessel had been handed over to her owners, the workforce at the shipyard would at last have time to wave good-bye to her and wish her God speed.

Titanic at outfitting wharf.

(Ulster Folk and Transport Museum. Photograph reproduced courtesy the Trustees of National Museums Northern Ireland)

42

Detail from Belfast Newsletter *30 May 1911, announcing the launch of the* Titanic.

CHAPTER 5

The Launch of the *Titanic*

Wednesday, 31 May 1911 was a special day, both for Harland and Wolff and for the White Star Line. On that day, the *Olympic* was to be handed over to the White Star Line, and *SS 401*, the *Titanic*, was to be launched.

A week before the launch, the *Belfast Newsletter* carried an advertisement from Mr W.A. Currie, Secretary to the Belfast Harbour Commissioners, stating that the Victoria wharf would be closed for all shipping movements on 31 May from 10.00 a.m. until after the *Titanic* had been berthed.

On 24 May and again on 30 May, the *Newsletter* carried an advertisement for the launch of the *Titanic* (see opposite). Tickets could be purchased for one shilling; however, if they were purchased on or before 30 May, the cost would be nine old pence for adults and six old pence for children. These tickets guaranteed holders a place in a specially reserved enclosure at the Albert Quay, from which they would have a clear view of the proceedings. Tickets could be bought from various Belfast shops, including Thortons, Leahy Kelly and Leahy, Jordons and various music shops.

The *Belfast Newsletter* also stated that extra trams from Castle Junction to Pilot Street at Queen's Quay would be provided by the Belfast Corporation, starting at 10.30 a.m., to accommodate the thousands of spectators who were expected to watch the launch. Extra ferries were also provided from the Abercorn and Milewater Basin.

The tickets purchased by members of the public were printed on paper; they were perforated and numbered, and the White Star flag was printed on them in red. The proceeds from the sale of the tickets went to the Queen Street Hospital and to the children's hospital at Templemore Avenue, Belfast. Not all of the spectators, however, would have needed to buy their tickets. White-collar workers at the shipyard were given invitations that allowed them into the enclosure at the slipway. These special tickets were printed on card, they were not numbered and had no perforations. The White Star flag was printed on them in red. The example shown here (page 44) was given to Mr J. Cuming of St Vincent Street, Belfast. Mr Cuming worked in the time office at the shipyard; as a timekeeper, he probably knew the majority of the workers, and from the time office he would have had a grandstand view of the construction of both the *Olympic* and the *Titanic*. Receiving this invitation was a great honour for him. He kept the card after the launch, signed the back of it and passed it on to his daughter Lilly.

Launch ticket. Given out by Harland and Wolff. (Author's collection)

Not all the members of the shipyard's workforce would have been able to attend the launch of the *Titanic*. In May 1910, the managing directors of the shipyard had issued the following instructions with regard to any future launchings:

> NOTICE
> After this date any of the staff or their friends wishing to witness a launch must send in an application on a Question and Answer reply form, the day prior to the launch, to his Superior, unless he has an actual duty to perform in connection with the said launch and has instructions either from his Superior or from one of the Managing Directors.
>   Any violation of this rule will mean dismissal.
> *26th May 1910*[1]

It is believed that any members of the shipyard workforce who attended a launch were not paid for the period of the ceremony.

The day of the *Titanic*'s launch, 31 May 1911, was a glorious one. The list of distinguished guests included Lord and Lady Pirrie (both of whom celebrated their birthday on that day); J. Pierpoint Morgan, the American owner of the International Mercantile Marine Company, which owned the White Star Line; J. Bruce Ismay, the Chairman of the White Star Line, and members of his family; Mr Sanderson, director and manager of the White Star Line; Thomas Andrews of Harland and

Wolff; Commander Holland; and the Lord and Lady Mayoress of Belfast, Mr and Mrs McMordie.

At 11.00 a.m., the gates to the stands were opened to allow the spectators to enter. The owners' gallery had been set up on the port side of the *Titanic*, and was draped in white and crimson. Three other stands had been erected at the end of the shipyard opposite the bows of the ship. One was reserved for the hundreds of journalists who had travelled from as far away as London and America to report on the event; the other two stands were for ticket-holders (including Mr J. Cuming). These ticket-holders had to be in their seats in the Harland and Wolff stands before noon, when a rocket was fired to signal that the launching was imminent, and to warn any small craft in the water near the launch site to pull away. At 12.10 p.m. a second rocket signalled that the gates were being shut and that there would be no further admittance.

While this was happening, Lord Pirrie made his way from the owners' stand and began his final inspection of the ship. He walked along both sides of the ship, ensuring that all the wooden props had been removed. He also made a final inspection of the launching equipment. Finally, Pirrie gave the signal for the third rocket to be fired and the *Titanic* to be launched.

The White Star Line's flag flew over the bow of the ship, and flags were hung spelling out the word 'SUCCESS'.

Lord Pirrie and J. Bruce Ismay at the launch of the Titanic.

(Ulster Folk and Transport Museum. Photograph reproduced courtesy the Trustees of National Museums Northern Ireland)

No one broke a bottle of champagne over the *Titanic*'s bow, or uttered the words 'May God bless her....' However, there is a report that Mrs Bruce Ismay said quietly, from her seat in the spectators' stand, 'I name this ship the *Titanic*, and may God bless her and all who sail in her.'[2]

Thirteen minutes after midday, the *Titanic* was released from her position on the slipway by the hydraulic launching ram and started her way down the slip. She was in motion for the first time. The *Newsletter* reported: 'She took to the water as though she was eager for the baptism, and in a short space of 62 seconds she was entirely free of the way.'[3]

On each side of the Lagan, great anchors had previously been set in the river bed by the 150 ton floating crane; their steel hawsers were fastened to eye-plates on board the ship. The Titanic was pulled to a halt in less than one half of her own length.

The men watching the ceremony pulled off their caps and hats and shouted themselves hoarse, while the large number of ladies waved their handkerchiefs excitedly. Gradually the cheering stopped, and fifteen minutes after the *Titanic* had come to a stop in the water, the crowds of many thousands had already dwindled away.

The launch weight of the *Titanic* was between 25,000 and 26,000 tons. Within one hour of the launch, the *Titanic* had been towed to the outfitting wharf and berthed.

Lunch was provided for the distinguished guests at Queens Island, while the press and other guests — unfortunately, without Lord and Lady Pirrie — dined at the Grand Central Hotel in Royal Avenue, Belfast.

Because of White Star Line policy, no one officially had the honour of christening the *Titanic*; but a special place must be reserved in history for the person who was in charge of the hydraulic ram that gently released the great ship, starting her down the slipway and into history. This honour was given to Mr Charles Payne, a manager in the shipyard, who operated the ram when Lord Pirrie gave the signal.

The day of the launch was also a big day for one five year-old boy. Young John Andrews, the nephew of Thomas Andrews, was allowed, as a special treat, to assist in the launch by knocking away one of the many small wedges that held the *Titanic* on the slipway. John remembered this occasion all his life, and told and retold the story to his family and later to his children.

Menu for post-launch dinner.

(Author's collection)

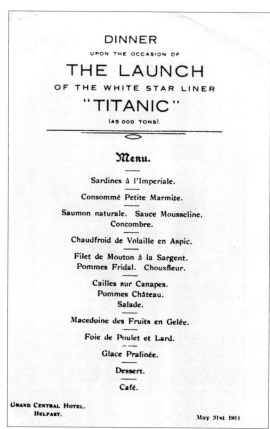

DINNER

UPON THE OCCASION OF

THE LAUNCH

OF THE WHITE STAR LINER

"TITANIC"

(45 000 TONS).

Menu.

Sardines à l'Imperiale.

Consommé Petite Marmite.

Saumon naturale. Sauce Mousseline.
Concombre.

Chaudfroid de Volaille en Aspic.

Filet de Mouton à la Sargent.
Pommes Fridal. Chouxfleur.

Cailles sur Canapes.
Pommes Château.
Salade.

Macedoine des Fruits en Gelée.

Foie de Poulet et Lard.

Glace Pralinée.

Dessert.

Café.

GRAND CENTRAL HOTEL.
BELFAST.

May 31st 1911.

CHAPTER 6

Ghostly Images

For many years, Harland and Wolff were aware of the need to photograph and record the various stages in the construction of their ships. Local photographers R.J. Welch and Alex Hogg became famous, not only for their images of Belfast, but for their records of key events at Harland and Wolff's shipyard.

Photography at the beginning of the century was very different from what it is today. Large, heavy box cameras using glass plate negatives were the order of the day. In general, the subject to be photographed came to the photographer's studio, so that the photographer would not have to carry the heavy equipment around. Over the years, however, Welch and Hogg made many visits to the shipyard to record the construction of the ships.

Sometimes, however, all did not go according to plan. If someone were to move suddenly or if there was too much activity while the photograph was being taken, the picture on the negative could become distorted, leaving a ghostly image.

A close examination of photographs of the *Olympic* and the *Titanic* reveals that many of the negatives — especially those of the *Titanic* — appear to have been altered, leaving behind ghostly images in the final photographs.

It is a well-known fact that the White Star Line, unlike shipping companies of today, did not believe in christening its ships at their launches. Also unlike modern shipping companies, the White Star Line made no secret of the proposed names of its newest vessels: each ship's name would be prominently displayed on the gantry, in front of the growing steelwork and plating.

A photograph (No.1 on page 49) taken by Alex Hogg in 1910 shows the *Titanic* and the *Olympic* in Harland and Wolff's Arroll gantry, at slips No. 2 and No. 3. Two notice-boards attached to the gantry bear the words 'White Star — Royal Mail Steamer — *Olympic*' and 'White Star — Royal Mail Steamer — *Titanic*'.

This photograph must have been taken soon before the *Olympic* was launched. It shows the *Olympic* fully painted; her hull is white, and the staging around her has been removed. Most interestingly, her name, 'OLYMPIC', is painted on her port bow, in black against her white hull. The *Titanic* — seven months from her launch, and still under construction — is seen in the background, darkened by a wall of staging.

48

Alex Hogg (a well-known photographer of his day) was back at the shipyard on 20 October 1910 for the launch of the *Olympic*. He took a breathtaking photograph (No. 2, opposite) of the *Olympic* approximately 30 seconds after she started down the slipway. On the stern, in black, are her name and her port of registry: 'OLYMPIC — LIVERPOOL'. Both the name on the bow and that on the stern are clearly visible against the white hull.

A Harland and Wolff photograph (No. 3, page 50) taken in 1911 shows the *Titanic* still under construction; her hull has been painted black, although her port anchor is not yet in place. This photograph was taken from the front port quarter, looking up at the *Titanic*'s port bow, and also shows details of the Arroll gantry. The ship's name, 'TITANIC', is clearly visible on her port bow, painted in white against her black hull.

Picture No. 4 (page 52) is a close-up of what must be considered the classic *Titanic* photograph. The ship is sitting patiently in the slip, awaiting her launch into history; her hull is painted black, with red anti-fouling paint on the lower hull, and on her port bow, in white, is her name — 'TITANIC'.

Another photograph (No. 5, page 53) — also taken from the port bow, but from a different angle — appears to have been taken not long before the *Titanic*'s launch. Two well-dressed ladies are present; the temporary stand is in place; and an umbrella is clearly visible at the front right-hand side of the stand, suggesting that the first of the specially invited guests are in place awaiting the launch. In this photograph, close scrutiny of the *Titanic*'s port bow shows no name.

Photograph No. 6 (page 53) — taken after the launch by Alex Hogg, from roughly the same location from which he captured the launch of the *Olympic* (photograph No. 2) — shows a view of the *Titanic*'s port side; a careful check reveals no name on the bow. Another photograph taken by Harland and Wolff during the *Titanic*'s launch (No. 7, page 54) also shows no name on her hull. What happened to the name?

A further photograph, taken by the *Cork Examiner* (but not included here), shows the *Titanic* being fitted out — and raises yet another question. The ship's name is visible on her port bow — not in the bright white of photograph No. 4, but in a deeper colour, nearly black. The *Titanic* was also caught on camera as she left Southampton; again, her name is visible, but it is clearly not in white, as it apparently was at the launch.

There are, then, several questions to consider:

1. Why was the *Olympic*'s hull white and her name black at the time of her launch? Her hull was later to be painted black and her name white.

2. Why is the *Titanic*'s name clearly visible on photographs taken prior to her launch (eg. Nos. 3 & 4), while, in photographs taken only two or three minutes after the launch (eg. No. 7), the name appears to have disappeared?

1. Olympic *and* Titanic *in Arrol Gantry.*
(A. Hogg)

2. Launch of Olympic.
(A. Hogg)

Both — Ulster Museum Belfast. Photographs reproduced courtesy the Trustees of National Museums Northern Ireland.

3. Titanic *in gantry with anchor name visible.*

(Ulster Folk and Transport Museum. Photograph reproduced courtesy the Trustees of National Museums Northern Ireland)

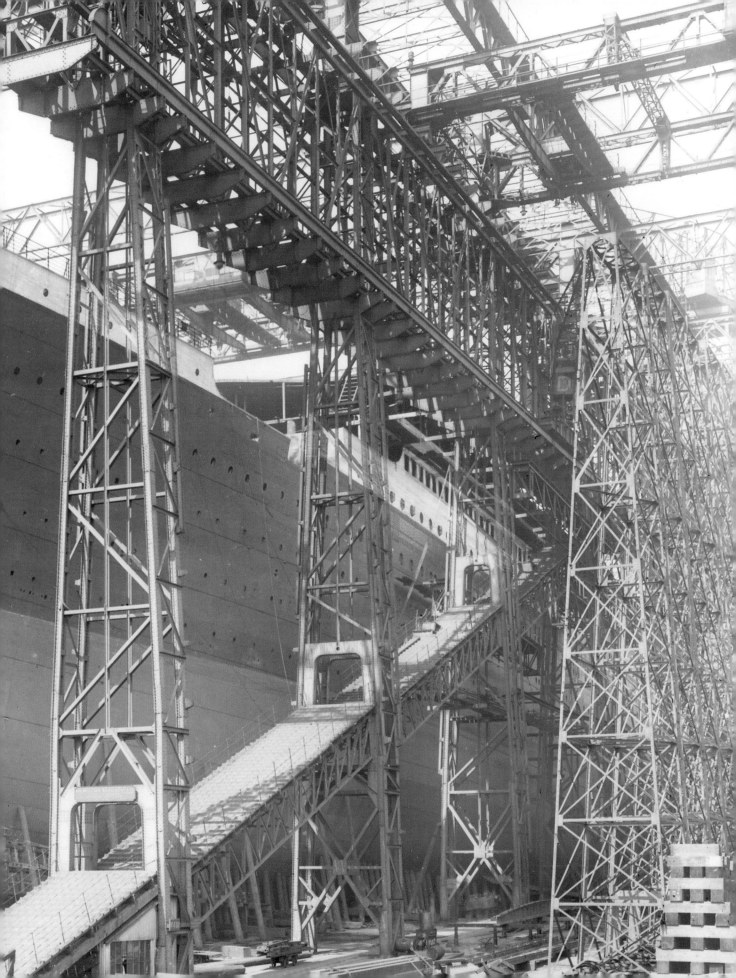

52

4. Detail from photograph of Titanic
in gantry with name visible.

5. Above: Titanic in slipway prior to launch (name not visible).   *6. Below: Titanic during launch (no name visible).*

54

7. Titanic after launch (no name visible)

(Ulster Museum Belfast. Photograph reproduced courtesy the Trustees of National Museums Northern Ireland)

3. Why, in later photographs, is the *Titanic*'s name a dull colour, as opposed to the white shown in photographs 3 and 4?

4. How was the name applied to the ship's hull?

To begin with Question No. 1: The *Olympic* was the flagship of the three proposed sisters; she was the first-born, the most special. Refinements would later be made to the *Titanic* and the *Britannic*, but Harland and Wolff were most proud of the *Olympic*. It was only when the *Titanic* sank that her fame eclipsed that of her elder sister; and the youngest sister never got the chance to shine. The *Britannic* never saw service with the White Star Line; she was press-ganged into service in the First World War, and was lost without ever carrying a fare-paying passenger for her owners.

Harland and Wolff wanted the *Olympic*, the first of the three sisters, to stand out at her launch. Her hull was painted white, to contrast with the gantry and with the *Titanic*, which was on the adjoining slipway, and to make her hull appear enormous compared with that of any other large ship. Her name was set out on her hull in contrasting black. She was the jewel in the crown, and she should look gigantic and pleasing for her launch. Later, at the fitting-out wharf and the dry dock, her upper hull would be painted black and her name white.

The *Titanic*'s name is another matter. It is often said that the camera never lies, and I cannot disagree. However, when the photographer's hand and skill come in contact with the negative, anything is possible, and seeing is not necessarily believing. Close examination of the original glass negatives of two Harland and Wolff photographs (Nos. 3 & 4) shows clearly that the photographer literally had a hand in the picture.

Photograph No. 3 shows the *Titanic* awaiting her anchor, with her name prominently displayed on her hull. Nothing seems to be amiss — until one looks at the reverse of the negative. The *Titanic*'s name has been pencilled in, and not very well at that. Two pencil lines, approximately 22mm long and 2mm apart, have been drawn as a guide for the letters. The cross-stroke of the N has been done twice, while the C has been drawn with the back curved instead of straight. Closer examination reveals a very faint T just beside the first T, to the left of the metal tower; and to the right of the final C, directly below the fifth porthole on the white forecastle, is a very faint second C.

The photographer, seeing that the metal tower was blocking the *Titanic*'s name, has moved the name slightly to the right and, in the process, has bunched the letters closely together. He has shaded the negative with a pencil, which would turn this area white in any print made from this negative.

Photograph No. 4 also shows the photographer's hand at work. Some substance — quite probably a rubber solution known as liquid opaque — has been applied to the reverse side of this negative. These alterations have been made with more care and attention than those made to photograph No. 3, but dab-marks can be clearly seen where the solution has been applied finely along the lines of the letters. In this photo, the letter C has a straight back and is placed underneath the fifth porthole in the forecastle. It is also interesting to note the two 'ghosts' in the lower right-hand section of the photograph: in front of the woodpile, two men have been erased by scraping the reverse of the negative.

Why were these alterations made to the negatives? I do not believe that the photographer had any intent to deceive. Rather, he simply wished to enhance the finished picture. The *Titanic*'s name was certainly on her hull for the launch, but not in white; it appears to have been in a dull colour which would not stand out well against a black hull. The photographer had to help Harland and Wolff to ensure that the name stood out clearly.

This was quite a common practice in those days. Another example of this type of enhancement is provided by the photograph on page 57, which shows work being done on the starboard propeller shaft of the *Titanic* in the Thompson dry dock. A workman who was standing in front of the shaft, second from the right, has been taken out. There are several possible reasons for this. Perhaps the photographer or the foreman disliked the man, or perhaps the man simply did not want to be in the picture. However, the simplest explanation is similar to the reason for the removal of the workmen beside the woodpile in photo No. 4 — they were in the way. In the photo, the workman spoiled the composition, and by removing him, the photographer gave a greater sense of the enormous size of the shaft itself. Quite simply, these men were in the way, and their removal would, and did, make for superb pictures.

The final question — how was the *Titanic*'s name applied? — is probably the hardest one to answer.

On modern vessels, the name can generally be applied by one of two methods. The cheaper option is to have the name marked out on the hull in chalk at the required position. These marks are then overlaid in bead welding, and finally the space within them is painted in the colour selected by the owners. The second option is to have the name cut out in steel plate; these steel letters are welded into place and then painted.

In the *Titanic*'s time, however, welding was just in its infancy and was not generally available, so the shipbuilder had two different ways to apply the name. The first option was to chalk in the letters and then have a painter carefully fill in the lines in the required colour. The second option was to have the letters cut from steel plate. These letters and the hull would be threaded (holes would be drilled in them, and then a tap and die set screwed into each hole to make a thread to take a bolt); each letter would be fixed in place with two or three small bolts, and then painted.

The passage of time has made it difficult to find out exactly how the *Titanic*'s name was applied. Very few members of the workforce of the early twentieth century are still alive to tell the tale. However, Tommy McBride — a member of the former Ulster *Titanic* Society — was born in 1905. At the age of six he saw the *Titanic* being launched, and he later worked in the shipyard. Tommy — who, sadly, passed away in 1997 — clearly remembered his early days in the shipyard. His brother and uncles also worked there; one of those uncles was a painter, and one of his duties was to paint the names on the hulls of ships.

Tommy explained that when the name was to be applied to a ship's hull, a bosun's chair, consisting of a piece of wood held in place with a rope, was dropped over the side of the hull. This was done while the vessel was still on the slipway. A Jacob's ladder, made from rope and timber was also lowered over the side, and a workman would climb down the ladder and sit in the chair — there were no safety-lines or nets in those days. Using a hammer and a centre-punch, this man would mark out the corners of the letters on the hull. For curving letters like Cs, he would mark straight edges and then add in a few marks to show the curve. The painter would then make the hair-raising descent to the chair, join up the dots with chalk, and fill in the spaces between the chalk marks with paint. Tommy recalled that his uncle told him that the *Titanic*'s name was a yellow or gold colour, to match the gold band that the painters applied around her hull.[1]

Work on Titanic's *starboard propeller shaft end, showing 'ghost' second from right.*
(Ulster Folk and Transport Museum. Photograph reproduced courtesy the Trustees of National Museums Northern Ireland)

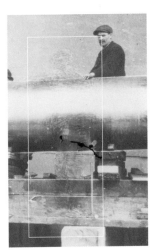

As has been stated, one of two methods would probably have been used to apply the *Titanic*'s name — either the letters would have been painted straight onto the hull, or steel-plate letters would have been attached and painted. In the negatives of photographs of the *Titanic*, there seems to be no evidence of raised edges in the ship's name. This may have been obscured by the tampering with the negatives, but it is probable that Tommy McBride's account does, in fact, describe the chosen method.

This assumption takes two factors are into account. Firstly, consider the expertise of the painters at the shipyard. Other photographs show men painting, freehand, very detailed wall-panels that would later be hung on the side of the hull of the *Titanic*. Secondly, consider the modern underwater film footage of the wreck of the *Titanic*. There seems to be no picture that shows her name on the hull. If her name had been in steel-plate letters fixed to the hull, it would still be visible, and it would surely have featured prominently in the pictures that have been released. Paint, on the other hand, would have dulled to the point of invisibility after almost one hundred years of submersion in sea-water.

The *Titanic*'s name was on her hull at the time of her launch. It was painted in yellow, by the workforce of Harland and Wolff, and enhanced in the photographs by the skill of the photographer.

CHAPTER 7

The Belfast Log

The *Titanic* was to leave Belfast on 2 April 1912 and sail to Southampton, where she would be officially handed over to her owners. Since about 1906, Southampton had been the main port used by shipping companies for the North Atlantic route. Prior to that, Liverpool had been used as the main port, this was where the White Star Line had its main offices, and also where the *Titanic* was registered. At noon, on Wednesday 10 April 1912, the *Titanic* was to set sail from Southampton for New York via Cherbourg and Queenstown.

When the *Titanic* left Southampton, she had on board a crew of 898, under the command of the White Star commodore Captain Edward John Smith, and approximately 936 passengers. She sailed to Cherbourg in France, where twenty-two passengers disembarked and a further 274 passengers boarded. At Queenstown, Co. Cork, her last port of call, 120 passengers joined her, bringing the total number of people on board to approximately 2,206. (The exact number will never be known, and it is still the subject of speculation and debate. The numbers quoted here are taken from the British Inquiry. However, even in the findings of the Inquiry, the figures do not agree. These findings include two different lists of figures regarding numbers of passengers and crew.)

The vast majority of those on board have been accounted for. However, no detailed research has been done on the subject of those who sailed on the *Titanic* on her first voyage — the short voyage from Belfast to Southampton, which she completed between 2 and 4 April 1912.

The *Titanic*, in her short life, had two Articles of Agreement, or ship's logs. The cover of the first one, which was signed in Belfast in late March and early April of 1912, states that it is a 'HALF-YEARLY AGREEMENT AND ACCOUNT OF THE VOYAGES AND CREW OF A SHIP ENGAGED IN THE HOME TRADE ONLY, and Official Log Book for a vessel exclusively employed on the coasts of the United Kingdom'.[1] This crew brought the *Titanic* from Belfast to Southampton, where, on 4 April, they were discharged from service. Over the next few days, the crew engaged for the voyage to New York signed a new log.

60

TRANS 2A/45/381 C

EXECUTED IN SIXTEEN PAGES

Eng. 6.
For 80 Men.

Any Erasure, Interlineation, or Alteration in this Agreement will be void unless made with the consent of the persons interested, and attested by some Superintendent of a Mercantile Marine Office, or Consular Officer.

Date of Termination of Half Year.

19

ISSUED BY
THE BOARD OF TRADE
In pursuance of
57 & 58 Vict., ch. 60.

HALF-YEARLY AGREEMENT AND ACCOUNT OF VOYAGES AND CREW
OF A SHIP ENGAGED IN THE HOME TRADE ONLY,
And Official Log Book for a Vessel exclusively employed on the Coasts of the United Kingdom.

☞ NOTICE.—This Agreement is to be used only for Voyages made on the Coasts of the United Kingdom, or to the Islands of Jersey, Guernsey, Alderney, Sark, and Isle of Man, or to places on the Continent of Europe between the River Elbe and Brest, inclusive. The Crew need not be engaged before a Superintendent in the United Kingdom, but all Seamen engaged at ports on the Continent where there is a Consular Officer, must be engaged before the Consular Officer. On whatever date the Agreement is made it expires on the next following 30th day of June or 31st day of December, as the case may be, and is then, or within 21 days afterwards, to be delivered to the Superintendent of a Mercantile Marine Office. If however, the Ship is absent from the United Kingdom on the 30th day of June or 31st day of December, then this Agreement remains in force until the first arrival of the Ship at her final port of destination in the United Kingdom after such day, or the discharge of cargo consequent on such arrival, when it is to be delivered up to a Superintendent.

On this Agreement and Account of Crew being duly completed and deposited at a Mercantile Marine Office, the Superintendent will issue the Certificate C.C., to enable the Ship to be cleared at the Custom House.

Neglect to deposit the returns within the time prescribed by the Merchant Shipping Act subjects the owner or Master to a penalty, and will lead to delay in the issue of the Clearance Certificate and consequent detention of the Ship.

The Master's attention is specially directed to the Instructions printed on pages 2, 3, and 4 of the Cover.

Name of Ship.	Official No.	Port of Registry.	Port No. and Date of Registry.	Registered Tonnage.		Nominal Horse-power of Engines (if any).	No. of Seamen for whom accommodation is certified.
				Gross.	Net.		
Titanic	131428	Liverpool	24/1912	46328	21831	6906	

REGISTERED MANAGING OWNER OR MANAGER.		MASTER.				FOR PARTICULARS AS TO LOAD LINE SEE PAGE 15.
Name.	Address. (State No. of House, Street, and Town.)	Name.	No. of Certificate (if any).	Address. (State No. of House, Street, and Town.)		
H A Sanderson	30 James Street Liverpool					

The Several Persons whose names are subscribed, and whose descriptions are contained herein, and of whom _____ are engaged as Sailors hereby agree to serve on board the said Ship in the several capacities expressed against their respective Names, which is to be employed[1]

In a voyage from Belfast to Southampton including trials.

And the Crew agree to conduct themselves in an orderly, faithful, honest and sober manner, and to be at all times diligent in their respective Duties, and to be obedient to the lawful commands of the said Master, or of any Person who shall lawfully succeed him, and of their Superior Officers, in everything relating to the said Ship and the Stores and Cargo thereof, whether on board, in boats, or on shore ; in consideration of which Services to be duly performed, the said Master hereby agrees to pay to the said Crew as Wages the Sums against their Names respectively expressed, and to supply them with Provisions according to the Scale printed on page 11 of this book. And it is hereby agreed, That any Embezzlement or wilful or negligent Destruction of any part of the Ship's Cargo or Stores shall be made good to the Owner out of the Wages of the Person guilty of the same : And it is further agreed, that if any seaman enters himself in a capacity for which he is incompetent, he is liable to be disrated : And it is also agreed, That the Regulations authorized by the Board of Trade, which are printed on page 11 of this book, and numbered[2] _____ and adopted by the parties hereto, shall be considered to be embodied in this Agreement.

And it is also agreed, That if any Member of the Crew considers himself to be aggrieved by any breach of the Agreement or otherwise, he shall represent the same to the Master or Officer in charge of the Ship in a quiet and orderly manner, who shall thereupon take such steps as the case may require : And it is also stipulated that advances on account and allotments of part of wages shall be made as specified against the names of the respective Seamen in the columns provided for that purpose : And it is also agreed, That[3]

the said Crew shall be on board this steamer on Monday morning, 1st April 1912; Firemen at four o'clock, and Seamen at six o'clock, and from that time until she is safely moored in one of the Southampton Docks they shall perform all work required of them by the Officers in command without any further payment than is entered against their names. Firemen to clean down after arrival as may be required. Food and bedding will be provided on the way round to Southampton; also tickets for the return journey to Belfast. Five shillings per day to be paid for detention in Belfast Lough, commencing from midnight, Monday, 1st April 1912.

In Witness whereof the said Parties have subscribed their Names on the following pages on the days against their respective Signatures mentioned.

45/381 C

_____ Master.

This Column to be filled in by the Master at the end of the last Voyage or the half-year.		To be filled in by the Superintendent.		
I hereby declare to the truth of the Entries in this Agreement and Account of Crew, &c. _____ Master.		Received at _____ the _____ day of _____		{ Superintendent of a { Mercantile Marine Office.
	19			

[1] Here the probable nature of the Ship's employment for the ensuing six months is to be described thus, " In the Coasting Trade of the United Kingdom"; " In the Home Trade." The particulars of each Voyage made under this Agreement are to be inserted in the Form provided on page 12.
[2] Here are to be inserted the numbers of any of the Regulations for maintaining Discipline issued by the Board of Trade, and printed on page 11 hereof, which the parties agree to adopt. Here any stipulations may be inserted to which the parties agree, and which are not contrary to Law.

N.B.—This Form must not be unstitched. No leaves may be taken out of it, and none may be added or substituted. If more men are engaged during the half-year, terminating on the 30th day of June or 31st day of December next, than the number for whose signatures spaces are provided in this Form, an additional Form Eng. 6 should be obtained and used.

[Sixteen pages.]

Half-yearly agreement and account of voyages and crew.
(Public Record Office, Belfast, TRANS 2A/45/381A)

When Harland and Wolff handed over the *Titanic* to the White Star Line, a crew had to be assembled to take the ship on the coastal trip from Belfast to Southampton. The members of the *Titanic*'s new crew began assembling not in Belfast, but at West Station, Southampton, at 2.30 p.m. on Tuesday, 26 March 1912, having signed on, on the previous day. Among the first seventeen to travel to Belfast were lookouts Frederick Fleet and Archie Jewell, who had both been transferred from the *Oceanic*, and who would be the first to spot the iceberg. The White Star Line apparently felt that these seventeen men could not travel on their own, as they appointed an officer to be in charge of them. The man they chose to supervise them, and also to sign on as the first Master of the *Titanic*, was fifty-one-year-old Captain H.J. Haddock. He signed on as Master of the ship on 25 March 1912, in Southampton, after transferring from the *Oceanic*.

In late March and early April 1912, the newly appointed crew of the *Titanic* started to arrive in Belfast. All the officers arrived, with William Murdoch being the first to sign on in the capacity of Chief Officer. Charles H. Lightoller, signing the log, gave his position as First Officer. These two positions were to last only until the ship reached Southampton. There, Henry T. Wilde was transferred to the ship as Chief Officer, which meant that Murdoch and Lightoller each dropped in rank by one position.

David Blair, a thirty-seven-year-old from the Isle of Wight who had just been transferred from the *Teutonic*, was engaged in Belfast as the *Titanic*'s Second Officer. This post was to suffer a worse — or perhaps a better — fate than those of Murdoch and Lightoller. When Wilde joined the *Titanic* in Southampton, Blair, instead of being demoted to Third Officer, was dropped from the ship's crew altogether. He was not on the ship when she left Southampton, and so he lived to tell the tale of how he was the Second Officer of the *Titanic*, if only for two weeks.

There is a minor mystery connected to Blair. It appears that, after he left the *Titanic*, no one on board was aware of the location of the binoculars for the lookouts in the crow's nest. One of Blair's responsibilities was to take charge of the binoculars supplied for use on the ship. At the British Inquiry, Frederick Fleet stated that, during the voyage from Belfast to Southampton, the binoculars were in place in the crow's nest. However, when the *Titanic* set sail from Southampton, there were no binoculars available for the lookouts. It was suspected that Blair had locked them up in a cupboard on the ship before leaving; Lightoller, who was to take over Blair's duties, was not made aware of this fact.

Members of the crew — including Third Officer Pitman and Fourth Officer Boxhall — continued to arrive in Belfast and sign on. Doctor William O'Loughlin, the sixty-two-year-old surgeon from Tralee, Ireland, transferred to the *Titanic* from the *Olympic*. Also transferring from the *Olympic* was the second Master of the *Titanic*, Edward J. Smith. The sixty-one-year-old captain took over the ship on 1 April, when he amended the log with the following entry:

> Capt. E.J. Smith RNR this day took over the command of the ship superseding Capt. H.J. Haddock RNR and signed the log Edward J. Smith, Master.[2]

2

Name of

PARTICULARS OF ENGAGEMENT.

Reference No.	SIGNATURE OF CREW.	Age.	*Nationality (if British, state birthplace)	Ship in which he last served, and Year of discharge therefrom. Year.	State Name and Official No. or Port she belonged to.	Date and Place of signing this Agreement. Date.	Place.	In what Capacity engaged.†	No. of Certificate (if any) and No. of Reserve Commission or R.N.R. (if any).	Date and Hour at which he is —
1	Herb. Jno. Haddock	51	Rugby	1912	Oceanic	25/3/1912	SOUTHAMPTON	MASTER	Comm. 7	
2								BOATSWAIN		WEST Southampton 2.30 pm 3/4
3	A Haines	30	Kent	do	Olympic	do.	do.	Bos'n Mate		do.
4	W. Wynn	41	Chester	do	Oceanic	do.	do.	Quartermaster		do.
5	M Weller	29	S. Hampton	do	do	do.	do.	Quartermaster		do.
6	J. Foley	44	Youghal	do	Olympic	do.	do.	Quartermaster		do.
7	A. Olliver	27	Jersey	do	do	do.	do.	Quartermaster		do.
8	A. J. Bright	40	Wilts	do	do	do.	do.	Quartermaster		do.
9	W. Perkis	36	Ryde	do	do	do.	do.	Quartermaster		do.
10	F. Fleet	25	Ryl	do	Oceanic	do.	do.	Look out		do.
11	A. Jewell	23	Bute	do	do	do.	do.	Look out		do.
12	H Jenner	31	Eastbourne	do	Teutonic	do.	do.	Look out		do.
13	G. A. Hogg	27	Hull	do	Dongola	do.	do.	Look out		do.
14	H Holman	27	Scotland	do	do	do.	do.	Look out		
15	G Rowe	32	Gosport	do	Oceanic	do.	do.	Look out Storekeeper		do.
16	S Hemming	40	Worcester	do	Olympic	do.	do.	Lamp Trimmer		do.
17	J. Hutchinson	26	Soton	do	do	do.	do.	JOINER		do.
18	A Nichols	42	Sydney	do	Olympic	do.	do.	BOATSWAIN		do.
19	W. M. Murdoch	38	Dalbeattie	do	Olympic	25/3/12 do	Belfast do	Chf. Off.		to
20	C H Lyghtoller	37	Chorley	do	Oceanic	do	do	1st Off.		do
21	D Blair	37	Yarmouth & Gw	1911 do	"Teutonic"	do	do	2nd Off.		do

† The capacities of Engineers not employed on the Propelling Engines and Boilers should be described here and in the Certificate of Discharge as Engine Drivers, Donkeymen, Refrigerating Engineers, &c.
‡ Should the Rate of Wages in any case be altered during the continuance of this
§ If the advance of wages is not conditional on going to sea, the
* If a British Subject, state Town or Country of Birth, and if born in a foreign
** If any member of the Crew enters His Majesty's Service, the Name of the King's Ship into which he enters is to be stated under the head of "Cause of Leaving"

The signatures of the original crew members — Captain H.J. Haddock, Chief Officer William Murdoch, First Officer Charles H. Lightoller and Second Officer David Blair — can be seen on the above page from the log.

(Public Record Office, Belfast, TRANS 2A/45/381A)

The last few days of March were very busy, with more crew members arriving, signing on, and learning their way around the new ship. The two Marconi operators, Jack Philips and Harold Bride, set about testing the new equipment and sending and receiving messages. Lookouts arrived — including Frederick Fleet, who would be the first to see the iceberg on that fateful night, only a few days later. Stewards, including Frank Herbert Morris, boarded the ship. The chief baker, Charles Joughin — who, after helping passengers to escape from the sinking ship, was to seek solace in a bottle of spirits, which may have helped him to survive — also came aboard; one wonders if he sought solace in the bars of Belfast. The engineers — from Joseph Bell, Chief Engineer, to Thomas Millar of Carrickfergus, Assistant Deck Engineer — appear to have signed *en masse* on 2 April, with their time to report for duty recorded as 'At Once'.

Storekeepers, stewards, clerks, greasers, stokers, firemen, room attendants, trimmers, a boatswain and able seamen all signed to sail on the first trip. In total, 280 men signed the log; it is interesting to note that not one woman signed on for this trip.

Oddly, no cooks or galley staff are listed. The log states that the crew were to be on board the steamer on the morning of Monday, 1 April 1912, with firemen reporting at 4.00 a.m. and seamen reporting at 6.00 a.m. The log states that food and bedding would be provided on the way to Southampton, but there is no evidence to show who was to prepare, cook and serve the food.

One other aspect of the log is worth noting: the deck engineers and some stewards signed the log themselves, but the vast majority of entries for the remainder of the crew appear to be signed in one hand. A possible reason for this is that the log was signed at the last minute. The purser, R. Barker, may not have been prepared for so many people to sign on at once, so he may have simply signed them all on himself. (It is interesting to note that Barker himself did not sign on.) Also, in 1912, literacy was limited. Take the case of John Haggan, a thirty-year-old fireman from Belfast. His entry, like the rest, was signed for him, and it has an addition: 'his mark', with an X between the two words. When John signed on for the voyage from Southampton, his entry was in his own handwriting, but on examination it is clear that he struggled to sign his name.

John Haggan's name and x mark are on line 5 of the Belfast log. His name is spelt with only one 'g'.

(Public Record Office, Belfast, TRANS 2A/45/381C)

64

Below: Excerpt from Belfast log, showing Captain Smith's signature (line 27).

Bottom: Excerpt from log, recording that the ship was carrying passengers.

(Both — Public Record Office, Belfast, TRANS 2A/45/381A)

On 1 April, Captain Smith completed the log. He stated that, as firemen J. Rowan and T. Gillen had failed to join, a J. Mullholland and a T. Holland had been engaged to replace them. Smith also recorded the *Titanic*'s draught and her freeboard measurement. He stated the ship's destination — Southampton — and recorded that the ship was carrying passengers and officials, among them the guarantee group from Harland and Wolff, led by Thomas Andrews. These men represented the various trades of the shipyard, and had been selected to sail on the ship's maiden voyage to correct any small faults that might occur. They were picked because of their skill and their dedication to their work; to be chosen was a feather in a workman's cap, and meant the chance of promotion on return to Belfast.

On that first trip there were 203 Ulstermen on board the *Titanic* — from Herbert Harvey, Second Assistant Engineer, to the majority of the greasers, stokers and firemen.

The *Titanic:* Belfast Signing-on Log (extract)

Name	Date of Signing	Position	Last Ship
H.J. Haddock	25/03/12, Southampton	Master	Oceanic
A. Haines	" "	Bosun's Mate	Olympic
W. Wynn	" "	Quartermaster	Oceanic
M. Weller	" "	" "	"
J. Foley	" "	" "	Olympic
A. Olliver	" "	" "	"
A. Bright	" "	" "	"
W. Perks	" "	" "	"
F. Fleet	" "	Lookout	Oceanic
A. Jewell	" "	" "	"
F. Jenner	" "	" "	Teutonic
G. Hogg	" "	" "	Dongola
H. Hohman	" "	" "	"
G. Rowe	" "	" "	Oceanic
S. Henning	" "	Storekeeper	Olympic
J. Hutchinson	" "	Joiner	"
A. Nichols	" "	Boatswain	"
W. Murdoch	24/03/12, Belfast	Chief Officer	Olympic
C. Lightoller	" "	1st Officer	Oceanic
D. Blair	" "	2nd Officer	Teutonic
H. Pitman	" "	3rd Officer	Oceanic
J. Groves Boxhall	" "	4th Officer	Arabic
H. Lowe	" "	5th Officer	Belgic
James Moody	" "	6th Officer	Oceanic
John Maxwell	" "	Carpenter	Majestic
William O'Loughlin	" "	Surgeon	Olympic
Edward J. Smith	" "	Master	Olympic
J. Bell	2/04/12, Belfast	Chief Engineer	"
W. Farquharson	" "	2nd Engineer	Oceanic
N. Harrison	" "	" "	Adriatic
G. Hosking	" "	3rd Engineer	Olympic
E. Dodd	" "	" "	"
L. Hodgkinson	" "	4th Engineer	"
J. Smith	" "	" "	Majestic
B. Wilson	" "	2nd Engineer Ass.	Olympic
Herbert Harvey	" "	" "	"

The *Titanic:* Belfast Signing-on Log (extract — continued)

Name	Date of Signing	Position	Last Ship
J. Shepard	2/04/12, Belfast	2nd Engineer Ass.	Olympic
James Fraser	" "	Engineer	Adriatic
F. Coy	" "	3rd Engineer Ass.	Olympic
C. Hodge	" "	" "	Teutonic
H. Dyer	" "	4th Engineer Ass.	Olympic
A. Ward	" "	" "	"
T. Kemp	" "	" "	SV White Lodge
F. Parsons	" "	5th Engineer	Olympic
W. Mackie	" "	5th Engineer Jun.	"
R. Millar	" "	" "	"
W. Moyes	" "	6th Engineer	Oceanic
William McReynolds	" "	" "	First Ship
G. Chisnall	" "	Boilermaker Sen.	Majestic
Hugh Fitzpatrick	" "	Boilermaker	Romanic
P. Sloan	" "	Electrician Sen.	Olympic
A. Allsop	" "	Electrician Jun.	Oceanic
Alfred Middleton	" "	" "	Demosthenes
Albert Ervine	" "	Electrician Ass.	Maloja
W. Kelly	" "	Electrician Jun.	First Ship
Henry Creese	" "	Deck Engineer	Olympic
Thomas Millar	" "	Deck Assistant	Gothland
A. Rous	" "	Plumber	Olympic
W. Duffy	" "	Clerk	First Ship
A. Foster	" "	Storekeeper	Oceanic
A. Khigler	" "	" "	Olympic
J. Coleman	" "	Steward	"
S. Blake	" "	" "	"
Thomas Curran	29/03/12, Belfast	Greaser	"
William Gibson	" "	" "	"
William McMullan	" "	" "	City of Cologne
Thomas Palles	" "	" "	Ivernia
William Burns	" "	" "	Olympic
Patrick Rogan	" "	" "	Duke of Clarence
John McErline	" "	" "	Ailsa Craig
John McTeer	" "	" "	Matener
James McIlroy	" "	" "	Olympic

The *Titanic*: Belfast Signing-on Log (extract — continued)

Name	Date of Signing	Position	Last Ship
William Gambell	29/03/12, Belfast	Greaser	Rion
John Cullen	" "	L.H. Stoker	Olympic
William Barnes	" "	" "	"
William Emnes	" "	" "	Rovenia
Samuel McGaw	" "	" "	Olympic
Michael Nolan	" "	" "	Ramore Head
Thomas Brennan	" "	" "	Black Head
Barney McKenna	" "	" "	Finhorn
Hugh Whinnery	" "	" "	Olympic
Thomas Murphy	" "	" "	Appichi
Joseph Beattie	" "	" "	Olympic
Stokes Barker	" "	" "	Braehead
Hugh Woods	" "	" "	Ramore Head
George Barker	" "	Storekeeper	Olympic
David Gorman	" "	Fireman	Torr Head
James Connor	" "	Greaser	Iona
John McGrogan	" "	" "	Olympic
Samuel Strange	" "	Fireman	Saintfield
Charles Kinstry	" "	" "	Zealandic
Andrew Shaw	" "	" "	Olympic
Samuel McGee	" "	" "	Francis
Patrick McGee	" "	" "	Olympic
Robert Bittle	" "	" "	"
Thomas Tinsley	" "	" "	Lord Charlemont
Robert Pierce	" "	" "	"
John Boal	" "	" "	Olympic
James Black	" "	" "	Lord Iveagh
John Cardwell	" "	" "	Cartago
William Bridan	" "	" "	Galway Castle
Nicholas Ferrant	" "	" "	Olympic
Adam Boyd	" "	" "	City of Belfast
Robert Fletcher	" "	" "	Lord Downshire
David McCarron	" "	" "	Olympic
Joseph Dunlop	" "	" "	Magpie
James Phillips	" "	" "	Fulmar
Charles McEntee	" "	" "	Buffaloe

The *Titanic*: Belfast Signing-on Log (extract — continued)

Name	Date of Signing	Position	Last Ship
Barry McIlroy	29/03/12, Belfast	Fireman	HMS Africa
Thomas Bartley	" "	Room Attendant	Lord Antrim
John Keenan	" "	Fireman	Lantcan
George Hall	" "	" "	Maggie Bennett
William Keenan	" "	" "	Olympic
William Keenan	" "	" "	St Stephen
Daniel Mullholland	" "	" "	Romanic
Patrick Cullen	" "	" "	Kelpic
David Kernaghan	" "	" "	Heroic
Thomas McMillen	" "	" "	Etterick
John Hale	" "	" "	Dunard
William Ward	" "	" "	Glen Head
George Hutton	" "	" "	Howth Head
David Lowery	" "	" "	Lord Charlemont
William McMillan	" "	" "	Duke of Connaught
Thomas Croskery	" "	" "	Innishowen Head
John Hadley	" "	" "	Duke of Connaught
James Stevenson	" "	" "	Olympic
William McQuillan	" "	" "	St Dunstan
Robert Cochrane	" "	" "	Eveyln
William Chevers	" "	" "	Dover
John Stevenson	" "	" "	Magpie
Frank McGough	" "	" "	Black Head
William Jameson	" "	" "	Olympic
John McGill	" "	" "	Innshowen Head
Archibold Andrews	" "	" "	Whitehead
Hugh McAllister	" "	" "	Devonshire
John Quinn	" "	" "	Iroquois
Michael Flinn	" "	" "	Lord Dufferin
Thomas Graham	" "	" "	Howth Head
John Craig	" "	" "	HMS Musgrave
Patrick Welsh	" "	" "	Olympic
George McDonald	" "	" "	Lackawanna
William Hanley	" "	" "	Graphic
James Massey	" "	" "	Cardiff
David Craig	" "	" "	Antrim

The *Titanic*: Belfast Signing-on Log (extract — continued)

Name	Date of Signing	Position	Last Ship
Thomas McBarty	29/03/12, Belfast	Fireman	Polo
John Hagan	" "	" "	Brayhead
William Miller	" "	" "	Saxon
John Denver	" "	" "	Whitehead
James Cleland	" "	" "	Atlas
William Swarbrick	" "	" "	Heroic
John Farley	" "	" "	City of Malaga
John Martin	" "	" "	Torr Head
James Little	" "	" "	Glendun
Thomas O'Flannagan	" "	" "	Woodcock
Daniel McAllister	" "	" "	Olympic
Joseph Halpin	" "	" "	"
Charles Decker	" "	" "	Rion
Nicholas Holme	" "	" "	Kathleen
Michael Croughane	" "	" "	Massanda
James Walls	" "	" "	Olympic
George Ferris	" "	" "	Manchester Exchange
Richard Turley	" "	" "	Carrigan Head
Robert Woodmy	" "	" "	Olympic
Thomas Neill	" "	" "	Glen Head
Frank Burness	" "	" "	Dunmore Head
William Murdock	" "	" "	Brayhead
David Gass	" "	" "	Kathleen
William Philips	" "	" "	Olympic
William Hepburn	" "	" "	Egret
James Reid	" "	" "	Torr Head
John Smyth	" "	" "	Patriotic
David Bain	" "	" "	Craigsman
James Holland	" "	" "	Olympic
James Armstrong	" "	" "	Freeherbert
William Pidgeon	" "	" "	Duke of C'land
James McArthur	" "	" "	Lackawanna
Thomas Connor	" "	" "	Olympic
Robert Cairnes	" "	" "	Clifford
Thomas McGivern	" "	" "	Olympic
William Maxwell	" "	" "	Graphic

The *Titanic:* Belfast Signing-on Log (extract — continued)

Name	Date of Signing	Position	Last Ship
William McIlroy	29/03/12, Belfast	Fireman	Dunmore
Robert Barkley	" "	" "	Rion
Patrick Morgan	" "	" "	Carrigan Head
James Lewis	" "	" "	Egret
James Little	" "	" "	Whitehead
Samuel Harkin	" "	" "	Olympic
John Barker	" "	" "	Bray head
William Mayes	" "	" "	Olympic
Barry McGowan	" "	" "	"
William Gregg	" "	" "	Thelman
James Henry	" "	" "	Lagan
Samuel McMillen	" "	" "	Black Head
Patrick McMullan	" "	" "	Ferguslie
Peter McKinney	" "	" "	Olympic
Robert Hedley	" "	Room Attendant	Memroe
William Simms	" "	Trimmer	Olympic
Robert Malken	" "	" "	"
James Carson	" "	" "	"
William Benson	" "	" "	Heroic
Joseph Swarbrick	" "	" "	"
David Shannon	" "	" "	Olympic
Hugh Herd	" "	" "	"
Thomas James	" "	" "	"
Robert Bradley	" "	" "	HMS Neptune
James Barry	" "	" "	Olympic
Robert Wallace	" "	" "	"
William J. Cassidy	" "	" "	"
James Auld	" "	" "	"
William Flemming	" "	" "	"
Robert McIlroy	" "	" "	"
Matthew Stewart	" "	" "	"
John Crossley	" "	" "	"
James McIlwaine	" "	" "	"
John Harvey	" "	" "	"
James Waugh	" "	" "	"
Thomas Morrison	" "	" "	"

The *Titanic:* Belfast Signing-on Log (extract — continued)

Name	Date of Signing	Position	Last Ship
John Bryan	29/03/12, Belfast	Trimmer	Olympic
Alex Horner	" "	" "	"
Joseph Kirkpatrick	" "	" "	"
Richard McMullan	" "	" "	"
Thomas McGill	" "	" "	"
Joseph Ellison	" "	" "	"
Thomas Holman	" "	" "	"
William Bailey	" "	" "	"
William Kerney	" "	" "	"
John Stewart	" "	" "	"
Hugh Calderwood	" "	" "	"
Matthew Patton	" "	" "	"
Thomas Lytle	" "	" "	"
John Flack	" "	" "	"
William Cosgrove	" "	" "	"
John Cosgrove	" "	" "	"
William Taggart	" "	" "	"
Joseph Loughran	" "	" "	"
Francis Beattie	" "	" "	"
Andrew Stevenson	" "	" "	"
Thomas Gibson	" "	" "	"
Henry McGivern	" "	" "	"
Joseph Smith	" "	" "	"
William Meehan	" "	" "	"
Arthur Valler	" "	" "	"
Patrick Keenan	" "	" "	"
William J. Hamilton	" "	" "	"
Thomas Robinson	" "	" "	"
Samuel Munn	" "	" "	"
Richard McGreevy	" "	" "	"
Daniel McDonald	" "	" "	"
John Mathers	" "	" "	"
Thomas Sloan	" "	Boatswain	"
Henry Starkey	" "	Able Seaman	Navahoe
Joseph Harris	" "	" "	Donegall
William Thomas	" "	" "	Helen Craig

The *Titanic:* Belfast Signing-on Log (extract — continued)

Name	Date of Signing	Position	Last Ship
Joseph Mann	29/03/12, Belfast	Able Seaman	Glen Head
James Benson	" "	" "	Olympic
Robert Harmes	" "	" "	"
John Thomas	" "	" "	Helen Craig
James Bloomer	" "	" "	Olympic
William Kavanagh	" "	" "	Eshmore
John Benson	" "	" "	Whitehead
James Morrell	" "	" "	Rion
Walter Smith	" "	" "	Centurian
John Burns	" "	" "	Thelma
William Heddles	" "	" "	Lord Iveagh
Joseph McIntosh	" "	" "	Gem
W. McGonigal	" "	" "	Heralda
John Gracey	" "	" "	Valdura
Robert Hopkins	" "	" "	Whitehead
George Barker	" "	" "	Olympic
Daniel Millford	" "	" "	Dewdrop
Hugh Donaghue	" "	" "	Glendun
Samuel Robinson	" "	" "	Hurworth
Patrick McKenna	" "	" "	Duke of Albany
John McCartney	" "	" "	Whitehead
Charles Dennigan	" "	" "	Ailsa Craig
James McEnspie	" "	" "	Olympic
William Douglas	" "	" "	Scandinavian
Charles Hinds	" "	" "	Romanic
John McWhinney	" "	" "	Olympic
J. Mullholand	02/04/12, Belfast	Fireman	Troutpool
T. Holland	" "	" "	Olympic

CHAPTER 8

The First Voyage of the *Titanic*

Before being handed over to her owners, each new vessel was required to undergo 'sea trials' designed to test the seaworthiness of the ship — her engines, her boilers, her navigation, her stopping distances and so on. The ship would also perform a timed speed run.

The *Titanic*'s sea trials were originally set for 1 April 1912, but when the day came they had to be postponed, because of bad weather and high winds. The firemen had been on board since 4.00 a.m. and the able seamen had arrived at 6.00 a.m. For the run to Southampton, the firemen were paid £3 each and the able seamen £2.15s. each; because of the delay, they were paid an additional 10s. per day as detention pay.

When the morning of 2 April dawned, it was decided to conduct the sea trials on that day. The representative of the Board of Trade, Mr Francis Carruthers, was on board for the trials, as was Edward Wilding from Harland and Wolff. Thomas Andrews was also on board, with the local members of the guarantee group: William Parr, Roderick Chisholm, Artie Frost, Robert Knight, William Campbell, Ennis Watson, Francis Parkes and Alfie Cunningham.

Before the *Titanic* set sail, Mr Carruthers carried out a full inspection of the ship. He and Second Officer Charles Lightoller examined the lifeboats, all of which were swung out and lowered. Mr Carruthers had one of the anchors partly lowered and rehoused, and he and

Contemporary newspaper cutting, reporting on delayed sailing.

(The Belfast Newsletter)

THE TITANIC WEATHER-BOUND.

Probable Departure To-day.

The mammoth White Star liner Titanic, which was to have left Belfast at high tide yesterday morning for Southampton, whence she is to sail on her maiden voyage to New York on the 10th inst., was unable to make her departure owing to the strong north-westerly wind which prevailed. Everything was in readiness for the sailing of the leviathan, but owing to the unfavourable weather conditions, it was considered inadvisable to make the attempt, having regard to the narrowness of the channel. Hundreds of spectators made the journey to the new deepwater wharf where the Titanic is lying, with the object of witnessing the departure, and if disappointed at not seeing her leave, they had the satisfaction of obtaining a good view of the vessel, which presented a magnificent spectacle. If the weather is sufficiently moderated in the morning the Titanic will leave on the first tide, Commander E. J. Smith, R.N., who was in charge of the Olympic since she left Belfast, being in command.

Lightoller also inspected the bulkheads and the watertight doors. The lifeboats were fully inspected. Fifth Officer Harold Lowe and Sixth Officer James Moody took an inventory of the contents of the lifeboats on the port side, and Third Officer Herbert Pitman and Fourth Officer Joseph Boxhall did the same for those on the starboard side. Pitman would later state that the lights missing from some of the lifeboats at the inspection in Belfast were in fact in the lamp-trimmers' store. He was quite certain that, at the time of inspection, no items were missing.

The *Titanic's* sea trials began at 6.00 a.m. and lasted for just over twelve hours. She sailed out of Belfast Lough and headed south into the Irish Sea, past the Copeland Islands and Donaghadee. A ship's sea trials would normally last for a complete day, and the usual procedure was to steam north out of Belfast Lough and sail towards Glasgow. However, because of the previous day's bad weather, this northern route was abandoned in favour of the quicker southerly route.[1]

The *Titanic* was set for various tests — she went from slow speed to full speed; she was put astern; her engines were put through their paces; she was put through a series of circling trials; she was tested with her port propeller going full astern while the starboard propeller was set full ahead. A speed run, where she reached speeds of up to 21 knots, and a full stop test were also carried out.

At around 6.00 p.m., the *Titanic* returned to Belfast Lough for the short journey back to Belfast, arriving at about 7.00 p.m. Mr Carruthers then completed his 'Report of Survey' of the *Titanic* (see opposite).

Before the *Titanic* set sail for Southampton, Harland and Wolff handed over plans and relevant documents to the crew.

Captain Smith was issued with the following set of plans:

Watertight Doors	Cargo Capacity
Fire Connections	Ballast Tank Board
Plugs in Ship's Bottom	Freshwater Tank Scales
Displacement Scale	Stability Curves
Docking Outline Plans	Rigging Plans
General Arrangement Plans[2]	

Chief Officer Joseph Bell was issued with the following set of plans:

Watertight Doors	Discharges Through Ship's Side
Fire Connections	Ventilation Plans
Ballast Tank Board	Pipe Plan Arrangement
Plugs in Ship's Bottoms	Telemotor Instructions
Freshwater Tank Scales	Steam Steering Gear House
Bunker Capacity Plan	Bilge and Tank Suction Plans[2]

Finally, White Star were presented with a complete set of all plans of their new vessel.

x. APPENDIX—*continued.*

DECLARATION TO BE MADE BY THE SURVEYOR.

I hereby declare :—

1. That on 2nd April, 1912, I completed the inspection of (a)_____ the steamship "Titanic," of Liverpool, Official Number 131428.

(a) If the survey was partial state what parts were surveyed.

2. That the hull and machinery are sufficient for the service intended and in good condition.

3. That the boats, life-saving appliances, lights, signals, compasses, safety valves and fire hose are such and in such condition as are required by the Merchant Shipping Acts.

4. That the hull, machinery and equipments will in my judgment be sufficient until (b) 2nd April, 1913.

(b) Insert date or dates.

5. That the load to be placed on the safety valves should not exceed the pressure in lbs. per square inch stated on page 4 of this form, and that the safety valves have been adjusted accordingly.

6. That the vessel, as regards the hull, machinery and equipments is in my judgment fit to ply as a foreign-going passenger steamer.

7. That the vessel is in my judgment fit to carry the number of passengers stated on page 2 of this form under the conditions there indicated, provided there is no encumbrance of the space measured for passenger accommodation.

8. That the certificates of the master, mates and engineers are such as are required by the Merchant Shipping Acts.

DATED AT BELFAST,

this 3rd day of April, 1912,

(Signed) F. CARRUTHERS,

Engineer and Ship Surveyor.

Mr. Carruther's expenses ...	£2	18	1
Other Surveyor's expenses ...	54	10	8
Balance of Fee ...	48	0	0
	£105	8	9

I Certify that the sum of £2 18s. 1d., which is made up as detailed in the margin, has been actually paid by me for travelling expenses in connection with the survey of the Steamer referred to in this declaration; and that the sum of £48 0s. 0d. is also as fee short paid under the scale sanctioned by the Board of Trade.

(Signed) F. CARRUTHERS,

Engineer and Ship Surveyor.

Surveyor Declaration page from Ship Survey of Titanic.

Mr Carruthers was paid £2.18s.1d. for travelling expenses and a fee of £48 for his survey. The completed declaration was handed to Mr Saxon Payne, Assistant Secretary of Harland and Wolff, on 3 April 1912.

(© Titanic Inquiry)

Form St. 1.

In triplicate.   No. 1415.

COMMON SEAL OF COUNCIL
FOR TRADE.
Issued by the BOARD OF TRADE.

PASSENGER CERTIFICATE.

For a foreign-going steam ship.

Steam Ship *TITANIC.*

Owner, Managing Owner, or Agent, THE OCEANIC STEAM NAVIGATION COMPANY, LIMITED, LIVERPOOL.

Port of Registry and Official Number.	Registered Tonnage.	Name of Master and Number of his Certificate.
Liverpool, 131428	21831	E. J. Smith, 14102

NUMBER OF PASSENGERS AND CREW.

Number of Passengers.*			Crew.	Total Passengers and Crew.
First Class.	Second Class.	Third Class.		
905	564	1134	944	3547

NOTES.   1.—All passengers are to have the use of sufficient space on the upper deck of the vessel, and no deck passengers are to be carried in addition.

2.—If any of the space measured for passengers is occupied by cargo, cattle or stores, one passenger is to be deducted from the numbers stated above for every 12 superficial feet so occupied.

* 3.—On any voyage on which this vessel may be cleared as an emigrant ship, the number of passengers is governed by the certificate granted by the emigration officer for that voyage, and not by this certificate.

BOATS AND LIFE-SAVING APPLIANCES.	EQUIPMENTS, DISTRESS SIGNALS, &c.
14 Life-boats { of the aggregate capacity of } 9,172 cubic feet { and capable of accommodating } 915 persons.	A fire hose capable of being connected with the engine, and of sufficient length to be used in any part of the vessel.
2 Boats ... { of the aggregate capacity of } 648 cubic feet { and capable of accommodating } 64 persons.	A safety valve on each boiler, out of the control of any person on board, except the master, when the steam is up.
4 Collapsible boats capable of accommodating ... ... 188 persons.	Compasses properly adjusted.
— Rafts capable of accommodating ... ... — persons.	Twelve blue lights, two storm signals and six small signal lights for attachment to life-buoys.
3,560 Life-belts or other similar approved articles.	One cannon and twenty-four cartridges or other approved means of making signals of distress.
48 Life-buoys.	Twelve rockets or other approved signals of distress.

THIS IS TO CERTIFY that the provisions of the Merchant Shipping Acts relating to the survey of passenger steamers have been complied with, and this vessel is fit to ply as a foreign-going steamer with the number of passengers stated above,

This certificate, unless previously cancelled, remains in force until the 2nd day of April, 1913.

A new certificate will be required before the vessel can ply with passengers from the United Kingdom after that date.

Dated this 4th day of April, 1912.

(Sd.) WALTER J. HOWELL.

Examined and Registered, (Initd) C. J. O. S.   *An Assistant Secretary to the Board of Trade.*

One of these triplicate certificates is to be put up in a conspicuous part of the ship, where it will be visible to all persons on board, under a penalty not exceeding TEN POUNDS.

If the number of passengers carried exceeds the number stated on this certificate, the master or owner will be liable to a penalty not exceeding TWENTY POUNDS, and to a further penalty for every passenger beyond the proper number.

Passenger Certificate from Ship Survey of Titanic.

(© Titanic Inquiry)

Appendix 1

EXTRACT FROM REPORT OF SURVEY OF AN EMIGRANT SHIP
REPORTS OF BOARD OF TRADE OFFICERS

1. A passenger certificate is in force for this vessel, and no damage to the hull or engines have been reported since its issue. I am satisfied that the hull, boilers and machinery are in good condition and fit for the voyage. signed F. Carruthers 2.4.12.

2. I have examined the distilling apparatus, which is in good working order and capable of producing 14,000 gallons of cold water every 24 hours, and the engineers are competent to manage and repair it. signed F. Carruthers 3.4.12.

3. The fresh water on board is certified to amount to 206,800 gallons, and is contained in 7 tanks. signed F. Carruthers 3.4.12.

4. I have inspected the boats and their equipments, and have seen 16 swung out and lowered into the water. The lifeboats are in order and are conveniently placed. The distress signals and their magazine, and the other equipments, comply with the regulations and are to my satisfaction. signed F. Carruthers 3.4.12.

5. The various steerage compartments comply with the regulations as regards light, air and ventilation, and measurement for the numbers for which they are fitted. No cargo is stowed so as to affect the health and comfort of the steerage passengers. signed F. Carruthers 3.4.12.

* * *

At 8.00 p.m., on Tuesday 2 April, the *Titanic* left Belfast and set out on the short voyage to Southampton. She arrived at Southampton just after midnight on Thursday, 4 April 1912.

There were over 400 crew on board, including firemen, greasers, a storekeeper, stewards, bakers, cooks and Mr R. Baker the Purser. Also on board were the members of the guarantee group that was provided for each ship's maiden voyage. Harland and Wolff also had other workmen — including Joey Thompson,[3] a painter — on board the *Titanic*, giving the ship a few final touches as she steamed towards Southampton. These additional workers would later return to Belfast via Liverpool.

The *Titanic*'s journey to Southampton did not count as her maiden voyage. Her maiden voyage would start on 10 April, when she left Southampton — or would it?

It is generally accepted that a ship's maiden voyage begins when she has been handed over to her owners and sets out on her first journey with fare-paying passengers. When the *Titanic* sailed from Belfast, she had on board, not only

Extract from list of crew engaged to travel to Southampton, which includes hand-written note regarding pay.

(Public Record Office, Belfast, D2805/SCP/A/3)

crew members and workmen from Harland and Wolff, but also one fare-paying first-class passenger. The *Belfast Newsletter* of April 1912 stated that a Mr Wyckoff Derholf, aged sixty-one, booked a first-class passage from Belfast to New York. When the *Titanic* sank, he was among those saved. Mr Derholf appears to be the only passenger whose passage began in Belfast.

It has always been thought that the *Titanic* sank on a maiden voyage, which began in Southampton. But she travelled from Belfast to Southampton with at least one fare-paying passenger; and this means that her maiden voyage began not in Southampton, but in Belfast, on 2 April 1912.

CHAPTER 9

Belfast Remembers

The tragedy of the *Titanic*, and the loss of 1,500 lives, had a devastating impact on Belfast, the magnificent ship's birthplace. Not only had the workforce's pride in her been deeply hurt, but most of them had been personally affected by the disaster as well. Many lost family or friends; many streets in the vicinity of the shipyard mourned for a loved one, a close friend, or a workmate. Grown men were seen crying openly and unashamedly in the streets; disbelief and numbness fell upon the people as the news spread. *SS Titanic*, the pride of Queen's Island, was gone.

The great loss was commemorated on the Sunday following the disaster. Thousands of people attended their local churches, where they respectfully remembered and mourned the loss of the 1,500 souls on the *Titanic*.

Extract from Belfast Newsletter, 20 April 1912.

Belfast Cathedral

(pictured left — author's collection)

The Dean of Belfast, the Very Rev. C.T.P. Grierson, led the large congregation, which included Thomas Andrews' mother and many of his relatives. In his sermon, the Dean said that the bishop of the diocese regretted being unable to attend. Harland and Wolff were represented by Mr J. Kempster, Saxon Payne and Edward Wilding. The Recorder of Belfast, His Honour Judge J. Walker Craig, also attended.

The processional hymn was 'Rock of Ages'. The text for the sermon was 'Our Father, which art in Heaven' (Matt 6: 9). The Dean said that the hearts of the Belfast people were wrenched, homes were desolate, and widows and families of the dead found it hard to say 'Our Father, which art in Heaven'. This, the Dean said, was where faith and trust in God came in — they must remember that their Father loved them, and that God would be good to those lost.

The hymn 'Nearer my God to Thee' was sung during a collection for the widows and orphans. The service concluded with the organist, Mr Brennan, playing the 'Death March' from *Saul*, with the congregation standing.

May Street Presbyterian Church

(pictured left— author's collection)

The Reverend Dr Patterson preached at two memorial services, to large congregations. Speaking from the pulpit, which was heavily draped in black, the Rev. Patterson said that the disaster had been the topic of conversation throughout the civilised world. Flags, he said, had been flying at half-mast, and some people were inclined to look upon the disaster as a judgement from God. He said that it often took a disaster such as this to make man realise his responsibilities and guard human life. The disaster, he said, was drawing men's hearts together, unbuttoning people's pockets and enlarging their sympathies. He concluded by saying that God had not come down in judgement on the people of the *Titanic* — the Son of Man was looking in compassion on the poor widows. A collection was taken on behalf of the bereaved.

81

The Assembly Halls

(pictured below— author's collection)

An hour before the beginning of the service, the building was full, and hundreds of people were turned away. The service opened with the choir singing 'Nearer my God to Thee'. The Rev. Dr McKean delivered the address, assisted by other ministers who offered prayers. The Rev. McKean said that our land and the whole British Empire had been thrown into mourning, and he offered heartfelt sympathy to the people of the city and of the neighbourhood. He said that, despite the tragedy, the bereaved should look to God and the Christian religion, which offered hope and deliverance — they should entrust themselves to the love and mediation of Christ. God's great fatherly heart went out to His people at this time, the Rev. McKean said, and He would bring them out of the depths of their sadness and into a more abundant life.

At the close of the service the hymn 'Perfect Peace' was sung. The congregation stood, and the organist, Mr F. Moffat, played the 'Death March' from *Saul*.

Above: Left — Belfast YMCA. The building has changed since 1912.

Right — Ardoyne Roman Catholic Church.

(Both — author's collection)

Belfast YMCA

The doors to the large hall of the YMCA opened at 2.00 p.m., and before 3.00 p.m. the hall was so crowded that the outside gates had to be closed and hundreds of people turned away.

The platform was draped in the White Star Line flag and the Union Jack, and nearly all of those who attended were dressed in black. One of those on the platform was the father of Albert Ervine, an assistant electrician on the *Titanic*, who had perished in the disaster.

The opening hymn was 'God moves in Mysterious Ways', and Sir James Henderson presided. In his address, he said that the *Titanic* had represented the very latest ideas in shipbuilding and had been a triumph of the skilled workforce. He offered his sympathy to all those who had lost loved ones.

Mr D.A. Black, secretary of the YMCA, paid tribute to Albert Ervine, who had been in his Bible class. He said that Bertie gave light to those who were saved, and that the memory of his blameless life and of his heroism (it is reported that all the engineers reported to the engine room after the collision and kept the lights burning until just before the ship sank) would abide with his friends forever.

The Rev. Dr Scofield of New York addressed those present. Paying tribute to those who had been lost, he said that naturally his thoughts were also with his own church in New York. The closing hymn, 'Nearer my God to Thee', was sung, and the service concluded with the benediction.

83

Mission Hall, College Square North

A special service was held at the Mission Hall for deaf and dumb adults. The service was conducted by Mr Francis Maginn, who took Psalm 107 as his text. He dwelt on the greatness of God, the littleness of man and the certainty that even the very hairs of our heads are numbered.

Many people gathered to pay tribute to those who had been lost — especially to Thomas Andrews and Artie Frost, who had been old and tried friends of the deaf and who had done much to help them gain employment. John Simpson, the *Titanic*'s assistant surgeon, who was the son of a member of the Mission Hall Board, was also remembered.

A collection was taken, and the money gathered was forwarded to the Lord Mayor of Belfast. The service closed with the hymn 'Nearer my God to Thee' rendered in sign language.

Ardoyne Roman Catholic Church

References were made at both services to those lost on the *Titanic*. The choir used Tennyson's beautiful lines 'Crossing the Bar' as their anthem. The organist, Herr Werner, had composed a setting for this poem some years earlier and had dedicated it to Thomas Andrews' sister.

Whitehead Town

Two services were held in the County Antrim seaside town.

In St Patrick's Church, the Rev. Hamilton Bennett began the service by reading from the rite for the burial of the dead. His sermon was based on Corinthians 15.

In the Presbyterian church, the tragedy struck home. The Rev. Knox, who took as his text 'The Pilot and the Passage', had the sorrowful task of offering

St Patrick's Church of Ireland church, Whitehead.

(Author's collection)

84

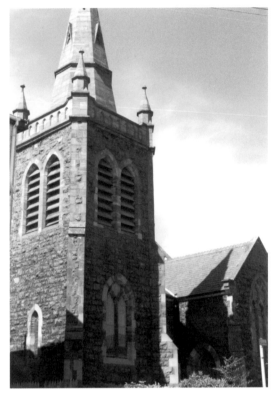

Whitehead Presbyterian church.

(Author's collection)

sympathy to a female member of the choir. This young lady had been engaged to Mr Harry Hesketh, a junior second engineer on the *Titanic*, who had been lost in the disaster. Mr Hesketh, who came from Liverpool, had many friends in Whitehead, and had last visited the town only a few weeks before the *Titanic* left Belfast.

Unitarian Church, Comber

On Sunday 21 April, the morning service was conducted by the Rev. Thomas Dunkerly, assisted by the Rev. Frederick Wooley of Belfast. In his sermon, the Rev. Dunkerly said that the congregation met with their hearts distressed by sorrow at the appalling disaster which had filled so many homes with woe.

The town of Comber had been the home of the noted Andrews family for many hundreds of years, and Thomas Andrews, who perished in the disaster, had been well-known and respected throughout the area. As his tribute to Thomas Andrews, the Rev. Dunkerly took the text 'Greater love hath no man than this, that a man lay down his life for his friend' (John 15: 13). The Andrews family members, who were not present, were described as pillars of the church. The Rev. Dunkerly recounted that the call which brought him to Comber had contained three signatures, one of which had been that of Thomas Andrews. He also told the story of how Thomas, as a young boy, in 1879, had rescued a kitten from a high part of the school roof, and had become the kitten's owner. Thomas Andrews, the Rev. Dunkerly said, was held in high regard by the people of Comber; he had ended a career of the brightest promise suddenly, but grandly.

At the end of the service, a resolution expressing deep sympathy with Thomas Andrews' widow and family was read by Mr F.J. Orr and Mr Robert Milling, and was passed in silence.

In Belfast services were also held at Donegall Square Methodist Church, The Grosvenor Hall, Rosemary Street Presbyterian Church, St Enoch's Church, St Thomas's Church, Elmwood Church, Belmont Presbyterian Church, St John's Church, Shankill Road Mission and Cooke Centenary Church.

Services were also held in Lurgan, Newry, Portadown, Antrim, Bangor, Coleraine and Lisburn.

The Hardship Fund

No one who was present at the launch of the *Titanic* in May 1911 could have guessed the fate that awaited this, the largest ship ever built. Less than a year after the launch, the *Titanic* had sunk to the bottom of the North Atlantic, with over 1,500 souls lost — including thirty-five men and one woman with a direct connection to Northern Ireland.

Two people who had been at the launch — Mr R.J. McMordie and his wife Mrs Julie McMordie, the Lord Mayor and Lady Mayoress — decided to do something to help the people of Belfast. On 22 April 1912, Mr McMordie held a public meeting at Belfast City Hall to officially open the Belfast Relief Fund, a hardship fund for the relatives of those lost on the *Titanic*. Notices were placed in the papers, and by the next day £5,471 had already been contributed. Amongst the many who gave were:

The Lord and Lady Mayor	£105
Belfast Ropeworks	£105
The Andrews Family	£330
Lord and Lady Pirrie	£2,100
Harland and Wolff	£1,050
Workman and Clarke	£100
Sir Thomas and Lady Dixon	£50

Whilst these large donations increased the fund, small gifts counted just as much; and contributions came in all sizes, from the Pirries' massive donation to 2s.6d. received from an anonymous 'friend'. When the fund finally closed on 17 May 1912, the Lord Mayor was pleased to announce that £12,896.1s.3d. had been subscribed. This money was to be used to assist the relatives of those who had been lost.

Belfast City Council

On Wednesday 1 May 1912, the Belfast City Council held its quarterly meeting at Belfast City Hall. The Lord Mayor, Councillor R.J. McMordie MP — who had been present at the launch of the *Titanic* — proposed the following resolution:

> That we, the Lord Mayor, aldermen and citizens of Belfast, acting by the Council, do hereby resolve that a record be made on the minutes of this meeting of our profound sympathy with the relatives and friends of the 1,503 persons whose lives were lost when the White Star steamship *Titanic*, after collision with an iceberg on the night of Sunday, the 14th April, 1912, went down in the North Atlantic Ocean. That we specially sympathise with those of our fellow citizens whose nearest and dearest were, by this gigantic disaster,

torn from them, and we pray that they may be sustained and comforted by the Almighty.

The City of Belfast recognises with unbounded pride that in the hour of trial the fortitude of her sons failed not; and while she mourns for her dead, she rejoices in having given to the world men who could so nobly die.[1]

Councillor James Johnston formally seconded the resolution, which was passed in silence with the members standing.

The Titanic Football Match

Following the loss of the *Titanic*, Linfield Football Club decided to play a special match in aid of the Relief Fund. Their opponents were to be Blackburn Rovers, and the venue would be Windsor Park, Belfast. In 1912 Blackburn Rovers were the English League Champions, and they had agreed to field their full team; so the people of Belfast would have a chance, not only to donate to the fund, but also to see the Rovers.

Linfield were to field a specially strengthened team which would include players from English teams. Everton's Billy Scott would keep goal for Linfield; he was quoted as saying, 'I shall be pleased to keep goal in aid of the *Titanic* Fund.' Sandy Craig, of Greenock Morton, said, 'I have permission from the Scottish Association. I am crossing on Friday night.' Marshall McEwan of Linfield, who would score Linfield's only goal, said, 'I shall play with pleasure.'

The teams were:

	Linfield	Blackburn Rovers
Scott	Everton	Robinson
Rollo	Linfield	Crompton
Craig	Greenock Morton	Cowell
Andrews	Grimsby Town	Walmsley
Harris	Everton	Smith
Stewart	Linfield	Bradshaw
Houston	Linfield	Simpson
Lacey	Liverpool	Latheran
McKnight	Preston North End	Chapman
McAuley	Huddersfield Town	Aitkenhead
McEwan	Linfield	Clemmell
	Referee Mr Bob Milne	

The match was set for Saturday, 11 May 1912, with kick-off at 3.30 p.m. Admission was a shilling for adults and sixpence for children. The gates opened at 2.00 p.m., and the Edenderry Brass Band entertained the crowd before the match began. The final score was Linfield, 1 – Blackburn Rovers, 2. The match raised a total of £173 for the Relief Fund.

TO-MORROW AFTERNOON.
" BE BRITISH,"
TITANIC DISASTER FUND.
BLACKBURN ROVERS
(English League Champions)
PLAY
LINFIELD (Strengthened)
AT WINDSOR PARK, SATURDAY, 11th May.
Kick-off, 3-30. Admission, 6d and 1s.
Band Promenade.   3965

Small ad from football section of Belfast Newsletter, 1912.

CHAPTER 10

The Belfast *Titanic* Memorial

While the people of Belfast were giving to the Hardship Fund, various people had suggested that Belfast should have a memorial erected to the dead of the *Titanic*. On 3 May 1912, Mrs Julie McMordie, the Lady Mayoress, held a meeting in the Lord Mayor's parlour at the City Hall, to discuss the suggestion. The meeting was well-attended, with Lady Whittle, Lady Byres and Lady Dill amongst those present. Mr F.W. Moneypenny, the Belfast City Chamberlain, was elected Honorary Secretary, and Mrs McMordie was elected Chairwoman and Honorary Treasurer. The meeting passed the following resolution:

> That this tribute to the memory of those who acted so nobly in the tragic circumstances attending the loss of the *SS Titanic* shall take the form of an appropriate public Memorial, to be erected on the most prominent site available, so that it may keep green their memory and serve to tell succeeding generations of their heroism and devotion to duty; also that the question as to its particular character be referred to a sub-committee for consideration and report.[1]

The people of Belfast gave generously to the fund for the memorial. By 25 May, the committee was pleased to announce that the fund had reached the sum of £1,035.0s.4d. Donations included:

Harland and Wolff employees	£231.5s.11d.
White Star Line	£105
The Andrews family	£360

Again, contributions came in every size — they included 5 shillings from 'a sympathiser' and sixpence from 'a friend'.

The memorial commission was given to Sir Thomas Brock RA, who had already produced two beautiful monuments that still stand in the grounds of the City Hall. The first, a statue of Queen Victoria, stands at the main entrance to the City Hall; the second, situated at Donegall Square East, is the statue of Sir Edward Harland. Sir Thomas Brock was also responsible for the statue of Queen Victoria outside Buckingham Palace in London.

The statue that he produced for the Belfast *Titanic* memorial is both a beautiful work of art and a sombre and stark reminder of the terrible loss of life.

88

The statue is, in total, over 22 feet in height, and is carved from the hardest white Carra marble. It consists of a group of four figures, set on a pedestal; the group is about 12 feet in height. A female figure — a beautiful piece of sculpture — dominates the design; she was originally thought to symbolise Fame, but she is now thought to represent Thanatos, the Greek goddess of death. At her feet are two mermaids rising from the sea (represented by the pedestal), bearing in their arms the body of a dead seaman. The figure above them holds a black laurel wreath in her outstretched hand, as if to place it on the head of the drowned man.

On the pedestal are two small bronze water-fountains shaped like the heads of gargoyles; they have recessed eyes and stumpy noses, and are framed by webbed antlers. It is thought that these creatures represent either Ymir, a creature from Norse mythology who fathered the frost-giants, or the Norse god Orgelmir, the personification of the frozen ocean, ice and fire. Water dribbles from the creatures' protruding lips into stone basins below the heads, and bronze drinking-cups are chained to the pedestal.

Engraved on the pedestal is the following inscription:

> Erected to the imperishable memory of those gallant Belfastmen whose names are here inscribed and who lost their lives on the 15th April 1912, by the foundering of the Belfast-built R.M.S. *Titanic*, through collision with an iceberg, on her maiden voyage from Southampton to New York. Their devotion to duty and heroic conduct, through which the lives of many of those on board were saved, have left a record of calm fortitude and self-sacrifice which will ever remain an inspiring example to succeeding generations. 'Greater love hath no man than this, that a man lay down his life for his friends.'

Also engraved on the pedestal are the names of the twenty-two Belfast men who lost their lives in the disaster. It is interesting to note that their names are recorded, not in alphabetical order, but in order of rank. Thomas Andrews, as managing director of Harland and Wolff, is listed first. When it comes to the crew, Archibald Scott, a fireman, comes before Hugh Calderwood, a trimmer. This practice of honouring the dead in order of rank ended with the First World War, and since then, memorials have carried names in alphabetical order.

While the memorial committee and the Belfast public were preparing to have the memorial commissioned, events were brewing in Europe, which would delay the memorial's erection and dedication for a long time. Eight years were to pass before the committee was ready to have the statue dedicated to the Ulstermen who had been lost with the *Titanic*.

The memorial was placed at Donegall Square North, in the road in front of Robinson and Cleaver's store, just in front of the underground toilet block. It was finally dedicated on Saturday, 26 June 1920, eight years after the *Titanic* sank.

The Lord Lieutenant of Ireland, Field Marshal Viscount French KP, arrived in Belfast on Friday, 25 June 1920. He was to unveil a stained-glass window commemorating the valour of the 36th Ulster Division in the First World War, in the City Hall, and also to perform the unveiling of the *Titanic* memorial.

On Saturday 26 June, the Lord Lieutenant was entertained to lunch by the Lord Mayor, Mr W.F. Coates JP, at the City Hall. At 3.30 p.m. he unveiled the window, and at 4.00 p.m. he proceeded to the main event of the afternoon.

The day was described as 'beautifully fine, with a clear blue sky and tropical heat'.[2] An area around the memorial had been set aside for relatives of those lost. The platform party included His Excellency the Lord Lieutenant; the Lord Mayor; the Moderator of the General Assembly, the Right Rev. H.P. Glenn; the Lord Bishop of Down, Connor and Dromore, the Right Rev. Dr. Grievson; the Lord Primate, the most Rev. Dr D'Arcy; the Earl of Shaftesbury; the Lady Mayoress; Lady Kennedy; Mr Charles Payne JP, representing Harland and Wolff; Mrs Julie McMordie CBE, who in 1912 had been the Lady Mayoress, and who had since become an alderman; and Frederick Moneypenny, now Sir Frederick, who as City Chamberlain had organised the proceedings. Sir Thomas Brock, the sculptor, was unable to attend due to ill health. Lord Pirrie was also absent, but he had sent a letter stating his deep regret at being unable to attend.

Once the members of the platform party were in place, the band of the Royal Irish Constabulary played the National Anthem. The hymn-singing was led by the Belfast Cathedral Choir, conducted by Mr C.J. Brennan. The first hymn was 'Why those fears? Behold, 'tis Jesus holds the helm, and guides the ship'.

The Lord Mayor then gave a speech recounting the events surrounding the loss of the *Titanic*. The Rev. Thomas Dunkerley read verses 23–30 of Psalm 107; prayers were offered by the Moderator; and the Rev. Henry McKeag, the Bishop of Down, read Matthew 14: 24–25, and passages from Revelations 21 and 22.

The Lord Lieutenant then unveiled the memorial and gave a speech. He quoted Thackeray: 'If we still love those whom we lose, can we altogether lose those whom we love?' He finished his speech by saying, 'In all life laid down at the call of duty, there is something imperishable — almost sacrificial.'[3]

The Lord Primate dedicated the memorial 'To the glory of God and to the

THE TITANIC MEMORIAL.

Lord Lieutenant and the Unveiling Ceremony.

Arrangements are being made for the unveiling of the Titanic Memorial in Donegall Square North at 4 p.m. on Saturday, 26th inst. It is hoped that the Lord Lieutenant (Viscount French, K.P.) will honour the city by performing the ceremony. The Titanic Fund was inaugurated by Mrs. M'Mordie, C.B.E., J.P., during her late husband's Lord Mayoralty, and she has since acted as chairman of the committee and honorary treasurer, with Sir Frederick Moneypenny as honorary secretary.

Cutting from The Belfast Newsletter *of 12 June 1920.*

90

memory of those from this city' who had lost their lives in the wreck of the *Titanic*, and read out the names inscribed on the memorial. The hymn 'Nearer my God to Thee' was then sung by all present.

Alderman Mrs Julie McMordie, Chairwoman of the memorial committee — who was later to become a Member of the first Parliament set up at Stormont — made a short speech, mentioning Thomas Andrews and Dr John Simpson. She stated that the events of the last six years, which had been so full of great calamities and heroic deeds, might have somewhat overshadowed the loss of the *Titanic*; but she hoped that the beautiful memorial would ever serve to remind future generations of the noble conduct, in the hour of trial and death, of those whose names were inscribed upon it.

The benediction was pronounced by the Rev. Dr Simms, and the gathering dispersed as the RIC band played the National Anthem. Following the dedication ceremony, Dr Simpson, the father of Dr Edward John Simpson, and Mr J. Millar Andrews, the brother of Thomas Andrews, were introduced to the Lord Lieutenant. Viscount French also spoke to several of the other relatives present.

In early 1959, it was decided to move the memorial from Donegall Square North, owing to the increasing volume of traffic, which was causing numerous vehicle collisions. Quite regularly, vehicles proceeding past the front of the City Hall either did not see the memorial or could not change lane quickly enough, and collided with it.

Belfast City Council let it be known that the memorial was to be moved, and set about looking for a new location for it. Amazingly, for a time, it seemed that nobody wanted it. Then various letters started to appear in the local press, offering suggestions for suitable sites. These included Madrid Street (the residence of a member of the guarantee group), Donegall Street, near St Anne's Cathedral, Albertbridge Road, the Old Shankill graveyard, Shaftesbury Square, and Arthur Street. The people of the small County Down fishing village of Portavogie even made a tongue-in-cheek appeal to have the memorial relocated there. The villagers felt that their small community would benefit from the visitors who would flock to Portavogie to see the memorial.

After much debate, the Belfast City Fathers decided to relocate the memorial to its present site in Donegall Square East. The memorial was moved on 28 November 1959, at a cost of £1,200 to the City Council. Now, set in the beauty of the City Hall grounds, the memorial is shown at its best.

In 1994, the former Ulster *Titanic* Society — of which I was then chairman — was approached by the Consark Design Group, which held the contract to restore the monuments in the grounds of the City Hall. Apparently, during the 1959 relocation of the *Titanic* memorial, the two drinking-fountains, shaped like little bronze gargoyles, had disappeared. The Society was asked to help in trying to trace them, and it was decided that my daughter and I would make an appeal on Walter Love's BBC Radio Ulster programme. Unfortunately, we were unable to discover their whereabouts. Consark made two replacements but the originals are still out there.

The following ode (author unknown) was published at the time of the memorial's dedication in 1920.

BELFAST IN MEMORY

It was my own men who built her, the mighty ship of pride,
To take the seas with strength and grace, a new Atlantic bride.
I sat, the lusty city, snug between sea and shore,
And clear above my clatt'ring streets, above my workshops' roar,
I listened to the iron's clang that sang how fast she grew;
My own men built her, heads and hands, they built her stout and true.
It was my own men sent her, the greatest ship of all,
To fight the seas for mastery and brave the winds at call.
There fell a sudden silence. My busy lough at gaze
Held breath to watch her stir and move and glide along the ways.
Then loud from all my people there rose a triumph cry;
Their thundered praise of her and me flung challenge to the sky.
It was my own men built her, the fated ship of woe,
That fell with snapped and maiden sword before an ambushed foe.
I sat, the stricken city, bruised between grief and shame,
Until I caught a healing thought to sear my wound with flame:
High among all heroic souls upon that death-bound deck,
Those men of mine who died with her snatched honour from the wreck.
Those men of mine who sailed with her and share her trackless grave,
Send home to mend my tattered pride the glory of the brave.
I weep, the mother city, unshamed to all the world;
My own men wrought, my own men died, my flag is yet unfurled.
And proudly in my proudest place be set my people's sign
How gain was wrested out of loss and courage still is mine.

CHAPTER 10

The Human Connection

The Belfast *Titanic* memorial must be the starting point for any research on the Ulstermen lost with the great ship. Engraved on the pedestal of the memorial are the names of the Belfast dead, in order of importance. (This practice of naming people in order of importance was customary at the time; it began to change during the First World War, when those lost were commemorated by regiment and then in alphabetical order.) When the memorial was dedicated, it was thought that only twenty-two Ulstermen had been lost when the *Titanic* sank. Their names, in the order in which they are given on the Belfast Memorial, were:

Thomas Andrews	Managing Director, H&W
William H.M. Parr	Asst. Manager Electrical Dept.,H&W
Roderick Chisholm	Chief Draughtsman, H&W
Anthony Wood Frost	Foreman Fitter, H&W
Robert Knight	Leading Hand Fitter, H&W
William Campbell	Apprentice Joiner, H&W
Ennis H. Watson	Apprentice Electrician, H&W
Francis Parkes	Apprentice Plumber, H&W
Alfred F. Cunningham	Apprentice Fitter, H&W
Herbert G. Harvey	Junior Assistant Engineer, Crew
Albert G. Ervine	Assistant Electrician, Crew
John E. Simpson	Assistant Ship's Surgeon, Crew
William McReynolds	Junior Sixth Engineer, Crew
Henry P. Creese	Deck Engineer, Crew
Thomas Millar	Assistant Deck Engineer, Crew
Hugh Fitzpatrick	Assistant Boilermaker, Crew
Joseph Beattie	Greaser, Crew
Matthew Leonard	Steward, Crew
Archibald Scott	Fireman, Crew
Hugh Calderwood	Trimmer, Crew
Richard Turley	Fireman, Crew
William McQuillan	Fireman, Crew

These names would mean very little to the casual passer-by. Thomas Andrews is perhaps the most famous and the most recognisable; but who were Alfred Cunningham, Thomas Millar and Anthony Wood Frost? Much detailed research has been carried out on the rich and famous who sailed on the *Titanic*; but what of those twenty-two men whose names are carved on the Belfast memorial? Who were they? Were they the only ones on board with an Ulster connection?

I decided to do my utmost to find answers to these questions, and to find out more about these men, their lives and their families. This was to be one of the hardest tasks I have ever set myself.

To date, I have found thirty-six people connected with Ulster who sailed on the *Titanic* on her maiden voyage. Twenty-eight of them died on that fateful night; eight survived to tell the tale.

There are six men with connections to Ulster who died when the *Titanic* went down, but whose names are not among those engraved on the Belfast memorial. These men were:

J. Blaney	Fireman, Crew
John Harper	Second-Class Passenger
James Heslim	Trimmer, Crew
Thomas R. Morrow	Third-Class Passenger
James McGrady	Fireman, Crew
W. Swann	Bedroom Steward, Crew

The people I have included must meet at least one of four criteria. Each one must:

· have an Ulster address

· be a native of Ulster

· be well known in Ulster, or have worked in Ulster.

Here, listed in alphabetical order, are the names of the thirty-six people with Ulster connections who sailed on the *Titanic*. Those shown in capitals survived.

Thomas Andrews Jr	Anthony Wood Frost	William McQuillan
Joseph Beattie	THOMAS GRAHAM	Thomas Millar
J. Blaney	JOHN HAGGAN	WILLIAM MURDOCH
Hugh Calderwood	Herbert G. Harvey	Francis Parkes
William Campbell	James Heslim	William H.M. Parr
Roderick Chisholm	ROBERT HOPKINS	Archibald Scott
JOHN COLLINS	John Harper (Pastor)	WILFRED SEWARD
Henry P. Creese	Robert Knight	John E. Simpson MD
Alfred F. Cunningham	Matthew Leonard	MARY SLOAN
THOMAS DILLON	Thomas R. Morrow	W. Swann
Albert G. Ervine	James McGrady	Richard Turley
Hugh Fitzpatrick	William McReynolds	Ennis H. Watson

Thomas Andrews
(LOST)

On 19 April 1912, Thomas Andrews Sr gathered the staff and servants of the Andrews family home — Ardara, in Comber — at the bottom of the main staircase of the house. He addressed them from the landing, informing them that he had just received a telegram from his wife's cousin, Mr James Montgomery of New York. Montgomery had interviewed survivors of the *Titanic* disaster for any news of Thomas Andrews Jr. The telegram read:

> INTERVIEW *TITANIC*'S OFFICERS. ALL UNANIMOUS THAT ANDREWS HEROIC UNTO DEATH, THINKING ONLY SAFETY OTHERS. EXTEND HEARTFELT SYMPATHY TO ALL.[1]

Thomas — or Tommy, as he was known to his family — had been born on 7 February 1873, into one of the most noted of Ulster families. The Andrews family traces its ancestry back to a Thomas Andrews, born in 1698, who settled in Comber and founded a mill for grinding corn. Ever since that date, the family has been connected with either feed mills or linen mills. The Andrews family has, throughout the years, been an extremely influential force in Ulster society; an uncle of Thomas's was a judge of the High Court, and his brother John would later become Prime Minister of Northern Ireland.

Tommy joined Harland and Wolff in 1889, at the age of sixteen, straight from his schooling at the Royal Belfast Academical Institute. Lord Pirrie, the owner of the shipyard, was his uncle, but Tommy did not enter the shipyard in an elevated position; he started as a premium apprentice.

During those early years Thomas travelled to Belfast every morning to work in the shipyard. He threw himself into his work, and also attended evening classes in machine and freehand drawing, naval architecture and applied mechanics.

When he finished his apprenticeship, Thomas was appointed an outside manager. He was then given charge of the repair department, where his ability was fully tested.

Below: Thomas, Helen and Elizabeth Andrews at Ardara House, Comber.

(Andrews Collection)

He was responsible for the lengthening of the Union Castle liner *Scot* (she had to be cut in two to increase her length by 50 feet). Thomas was also in charge of a similar operation with the *August Victoria*, and he supervised the reconstruction of the hull and bottom of the *SS China*.

In 1901, at the age of twenty-eight, he was made manager of the construction works. It was around this time that he became involved with the construction of the White Star liners, including the *Celtic*, the *Cedric*, the *Baltic* and the *Adriatic*. He was also involved in the construction of the *Nieuw Amsterdam* and the *Rotterdam*, for the Holland-America Line, and of the Red Star's *Lapland*. It was stated that he had immense faith in the new breed of large liners that Harland and Wolff were building.

In 1907 — as a result of his own achievements, not of his link with Pirrie — Thomas was made Managing Director of Harland and Wolff. By this stage, he was already deeply involved in the construction of the *Olympic*, the *Titanic* and the *Britannic*. It was said of him that it was not sufficient to say that his colleagues liked him — they loved him. He had an innate courtesy, and his chivalry made him unconscious of all class distinctions. Had he not perished on the *Titanic*, he would very probably have gone on to be Lord Pirrie's successor at Harland and Wolff.

Thomas married Helen Barbour in 1908, and they set up house on Windsor Avenue, off the Lisburn Road in Belfast. In 1910 they had a daughter, Elizabeth.

In the early hours of 2 April 1912, Thomas would have said his goodbyes to Helen and Elizabeth before making his way to the *Titanic*'s sea trials. There would have been no time to exchange goodbyes after the sea trials, for as soon as they were over, Thomas, along with the other members of the guarantee group, set off on the *Titanic*'s first voyage — the run to Southampton.

Sailing day, 10 April, came, and the *Titanic* set out on her maiden voyage. By all accounts, the voyage was extremely busy for Thomas; in fact, when the *Titanic* struck the iceberg at 10.40 p.m. on 14 April, he was still working on the plans of the ship.

He was summoned to the bridge by Captain Smith. This is not surprising, as his knowledge of every nut, bolt, rivet and passageway on the ship would have been far greater than that of anyone else on board. Thomas toured the vessel, and calculated for Smith how long he felt she could stay afloat. Thomas knew at once that the *Titanic* was doomed, but he did not panic. Instead, he helped others into lifeboats and assisted crew and passengers in donning lifebelts.

Thomas was last seen by Mary Sloan, who asked him if he was going to save himself. She said that he was more concerned with the safety of others than with his own welfare. The film *A Night to Remember* shows Thomas looking at a picture of New York as the *Titanic* starts its final plunge. We can only imagine the thoughts that must have been going through his mind. Had the ship been going too fast? If only the helm had been put over sooner, or if the ship had rammed the iceberg head-on.... If only there had been more time.... If only....

On 19 April, Thomas's fate was finally known. The telegram from New York was delivered to the offices of Harland and Wolff, and was taken to Comber by the man who had been in charge of the horse-team that had dragged the *Titanic*'s great anchor to the shipyard. The news devastated the Andrews family and the town of Comber.

Lord Pirrie later received a letter from a Mr David Galloway, written on board the *SS Lapland*, which was travelling from New York to Southampton. Among the passengers were members of the *Titanic*'s crew who had given evidence at the American Inquiry. Mr Galloway had been a friend of Thomas's. He had met him in Belfast, during the building of the *Titanic*, and had been waiting in New York to meet him again. After the sinking, Galloway talked to surviving crew members to find out the fate of his good friend. In his letter, dated 27 April, he said that a crew member had seen Andrews helping with the lifeboats. He had also been seen in the engine room with Chief Engineer Bell. Near the end, a young mess-boy saw Andrews and Captain Smith on the bridge; the mess-boy said that he saw both Andrews and Captain Smith put on lifebelts, and heard Smith tell Andrews, 'It's no use waiting any longer.' The boy also recalled that when the bridge became awash with water, both Smith and Andrews entered the water. An additional report stated that an officer said that Andrews was last seen throwing deckchairs and other objects into the water, and that Andrews' chief concern seemed to be the safety of others rather than his own.

Amongst the many letters of sympathy written to the Andrews family was one to Thomas's mother, Eliza, from an unknown mother. This lady wrote, 'I would be a proud and thankful woman if, when the day arrives for my son to face the portals of his life, I might have the joy of feeling he left behind him the unstained noble record of your dear son.'[3]

Helen Andrews, Thomas's wife, received a letter of condolence from the chairman of the White Star Line, Joseph Bruce Ismay. He had travelled on the *Titanic*, but had survived having found a place in one of the last lifeboats to leave the sinking ship. In the letter, he wrote that he had known Thomas for many years and not only held him in the highest regard, but also looked on him as a friend. Ismay continued:

> No one who had the pleasure of knowing him could fail to realise and appreciate his numerous good qualities, and he will be sadly missed in his profession. Nobody did more for the White Star Line or was more loyal to its interests than your good husband, and I always placed the utmost reliance on his judgement.[4]

He signed the letter 'Bruce Ismay'. The letter was written on 31 May 1912 — a year to the day after the *Titanic* had been launched.

Thomas was made famous by Shan Bullock's book on his life, *Thomas Andrews, Shipbuilder*, which was published a few months after the sinking. Shan Bullock was first introduced to the Andrews family in April 1912, by Irish writer and statesman Sir Horace Plunkett.

Sir Horace, the third son of the sixteenth Baron of Dunsany, was born in 1854. He was a Unionist MP, and would have known Pirrie and the Andrews family socially. In April 1912, he wrote a beautiful letter of condolence to Thomas Andrews Sr. Sir Horace wrote of Thomas Jr:

> Of the worth of your son I need not speak to you. Nothing I could say of his character or capacity could add to your pride in him, but you ought to know that we all feel how entirely to his own merits was due the extraordinary rapidity of his rise, and the acknowledged certainty of his leadership in what Ulster stands for before the world.[5]

Plunkett and other admirers of Thomas Andrews felt that something of his life should be recorded, and Plunkett approached the Andrews family with the suggestion that Bullock should write a book about him. Sir Horace visited Ardara on 11 May 1912 and discussed the idea of the book with Thomas Andrews Sr. Later that month, Andrews wrote to Lord Pirrie, telling him about Sir Horace's letter and asking for the shipyard's assistance with the planned book.

On 30 May, Pirrie wrote to Thomas Andrews Sr, agreeing to the idea of the booklet and granting Bullock access to the shipyard. Pirrie arranged for Saxon Payne to gather details on Thomas and to show Shan Bullock around the works. In the handwritten letter, Pirrie expressed his sense of loss at Thomas Jr's death:

> It was nice to see you all last Sunday facing up so well after the great shock it must have been to Lizzie and yourself and every member of the family.... I miss Tommy at every turn and it is hard to realise that I must do without his assistance just when I have come to rely upon him most.[6]

Pirrie signed the letter, 'I am, very sincerely, Willie.'

The book which Bullock wrote was made up of material, both from original documents and from Andrews' colleagues. It is beautifully written and paints a wonderful heroic picture of Andrews.

The people of Comber felt that some sort of memorial should be raised to Thomas, and it was decided to build a hall in his memory. Over the years, the Thomas Andrews Junior Hall has been used by many organisations and groups. Today it is an annexe to the local primary school, which is also named after Thomas.

Joseph Beattie
(LOST)

Joseph Beattie was born in 1877. He was employed by the White Star Line as a greaser, and his pay in 1912 was £6 per month. He and his wife, Maria, had three daughters and one son, ranging in age from five to thirteen years old. The family lived at 3 Isthmus Street, Belfast.

Beattie transferred from the *Olympic* to join the *Titanic*, signing on at Southampton on 6 April 1912, giving 'Sailors' Home, Southampton' as his last address.

On 21 June 1912, Joseph's widow, Maria, brought an application for arbitration and apportionment at the Belfast County Court (also known as the Recorder's Court) before County Court Judge J. Walker Craig. The respondents in the case were Ismay, Imrie and Company Limited. Mr Thomas J. Campbell, the barrister acting on behalf of Mrs Beattie, was instructed by the solicitors Donnelly and Company. In opening the case, Mr Campbell informed the judge that Joseph Beattie had lost his life on the *Titanic*, on which he had been a greaser. Joseph, he said, was one of those brave Belfast men who had remained at their posts and had given their lives to save others. Mrs Beattie, when questioned, stated that she totally depended on her husband's wages for herself and their children.

Judge Walker Craig made the following awards: to Maria Beattie, £96.13s.4d.; to Maria, the eldest daughter, £35; to Margaret, the second daughter, £35; to Agnes, the youngest daughter, £40; and to Joseph, the only son, £78.1s.8d. The judge also appointed Maria Beattie the legal guardian of the children.

In 1913, Maria placed the following poem in memory of Joseph in the *Belfast Telegraph*:

> I often sit and think of him
> When I am all alone,
> For memory is the only friend
> That grief can call its own.
> Like ivy on the withered oak
> when other things decay,
> My love for him will still keep green
> and never fade away.[7]

J. Blaney
(LOST)

Mr Blaney was a native of Ballycastle, County Antrim. He was employed by the White Star Line as a fireman, and was paid £6 per month.

Blaney, who was twenty-nine years old in 1912, signed on for the *Titanic*'s maiden voyage on 6 April. His last ship prior to the *Titanic* had been the *Harung*. His last address was given as 'Sailors' Home, Southampton'.

Hugh Calderwood
(LOST)

Hugh Calderwood was born in 1882. He lived at 6 Cargill Street, Belfast. In 1912, he was employed by the White Star Line as a trimmer, and his pay was £5.10s. per month. He joined the *Titanic* on 6 April, signing on in Southampton. It was his first sea voyage as a crew member.

His mother, Matilda Calderwood, brought a request for arbitration and appointment before Judge J. Walker Craig at the Recorder's Court in Belfast in June 1912. Mrs Calderwood stated that Hugh was her only relative and source of support. The judge, however, was not satisfied of this, and decided to let the case rest in case any other relatives made a claim.

In April 1913, Matilda placed the following poem in memory of Hugh in a Belfast paper:

No more shall the smile on his countenance brighten
the long lonely hours of one left behind.
But those who knew him shall never forget him,
His ways were so loving, so gentle and kind.
At the river's brink,
Christ shall join each broken link.[8]

William Campbell

(LOST) (pictured right — *Belfast Telegraph* 22/4/12)

William Campbell, an apprentice joiner employed by Harland and Wolff, was chosen to be a member of the guarantee group that travelled with the *Titanic*. To be selected for this group was seen as a mark of Harland and Wolff's confidence in an employee.

He lived at 28 Earl Street, Belfast, with his parents, was connected with Sinclair Seamen's Loyal Orange Order No. 1198, and also with Bethel Temperance Club.

In April 1912, William's sister, a Mrs Leathim, was on the point of death following a protracted illness. She wished to see her brother one last time, as she was devoted to him; but as William was travelling with the *Titanic*, this was not possible. The news of his death devastated his sister. She died on Tuesday 16 April 1912, with, it was reported, words of regret on her lips.[9]

WILLIAM CAMPBELL
(from photo taken when he was eleven years old), an apprentice joiner, who was one of the special staff on the Titanic sent by the builders, and whose name, unfortunately, is not included in the list of survivors. As already recorded, a sister of his passed away in Belfast a few days ago, and in her last illness was touchingly anxious to see again her young brother, who all unknown to her had met a cruel fate.

Roderick Chisholm
(LOST)

(pictured left — R. Boggs' collection)

Roderick was born in Dumbarton, Scotland, in 1872. He was the chief draughtsman at Harland and Wolff. He had worked for them at the Clyde works in Scotland, and then transferred to the Belfast shipyard in March 1892. At that point, his weekly wage was £5.6s.8d; by 1907 this had risen to £15.13s.11d.

Roderick married Susan Anderson in 1896, and they set up home in Jocylen Street. They had two children — Alyce, born in 1897, and Jimmy, born in 1898. Around this time, the Chisholm family moved to 6 Sandford Avenue.

By then Roderick had been appointed chief draughtsman at Harland and Wolff, and was working very closely with Thomas Andrews. Roderick was described as a very capable official, a man of great integrity, and a good linguist, and was highly respected by all who knew him.

As chief draughtsman for both the *Olympic* and the *Titanic*, he was familiar with the structural details of both ships. In 1911, he showed Mr A.G. Hood, editor of *Shipbuilder* magazine, around both ships. He was later presented with a cloth-bound copy of a souvenir edition of the magazine, and a letter of thanks from Mr Hood. Because of his detailed knowledge, Roderick was selected to travel on the *Titanic* as a member of the guarantee group.

Years after Roderick's death, his daughter Alyce recounted her memories of her father to her family. She recalled that, when she was a young girl, Roderick took her and her mother on a tour of the *Olympic*. Alyce remembered seeing Lord and Lady Pirrie strolling along the deck; she vividly recalled the feathers in Lady Pirrie's large hat.[10]

Alyce also remembered that her father was very fond of the *Olympic*, but did not like the *Titanic*. He did not want to sail on her, but as a member of the guarantee group he had no choice.

After the disaster, Thomas Andrews' mother invited the Chisholm family to Ardara, which Alyce described as a 'grand big house'.

Susan Chisholm was paid a pension by Harland and Wolff, and the company also paid for the education of her children. The directors of Harland and Wolff agreed to make a donation of up to £15 per child to pay the child's for education for one year. Depending on the results obtained, the company would consider repeating the donation in subsequent years.

The Chisholm family gives pride of place to several small ornaments that Roderick bought in Southampton, when the *Titanic* docked there after the run from Belfast. He had posted them home before he sailed on the final voyage.

Before he left Belfast on the *Titanic*, Roderick told his son Jimmy to look after his mother until he returned from the trip. Of course, he never returned, and it is interesting to note that Jimmy never married — he stayed at home and looked after his mother until his own death in 1960.

In 1912, Roderick and his family were close neighbours of another member of the guarantee group, Anthony (Artie) Wood Frost, and his family. Artie's widow, Lizzie, died in late February 1961; Susan Chisholm died less than twenty-four hours later.

John Collins

(SURVIVED) (pictured left — *Belfast Telegraph*, 22 April 1912)

John was born in 1894; he lived at 65 Ballycarry Street, Belfast, and came from a seafaring family. He was employed as a scullion on board the *Titanic*, and his pay was recorded as £3.10s. per month. He had previously been in the service of the Ulster Reform Club, Belfast. He signed on for the *Titanic*'s voyage on 4 April, at Southampton. It was his first sea voyage.

After the sinking, John was called to give evidence before the US Senate Committee. He stated that when the ship was sinking, he had been on the port deck, with a steward and a woman with two children. The steward was carrying one of the children. They were told that a collapsible lifeboat was being launched from the starboard side. John took the other child in his arms and carried it with him as they went starboard. When they all reached the starboard side, the *Titanic* was starting her final plunge. John was told to go aft, and was starting in that direction when he and the child were caught in a wave which swept them both into the water.

M.

Release on Termination of Service, with Note of excepted claims (if any).

Issued by the Board of Trade, in pursuance of 57 & 58 Vic. ch. 60.

Port Southampton

Name of Ship.	Name of Master	Name of Owner	Description of Voyage.	Commencement	Termination.
Titanic	E. J. Smith	White Star Co	New York	10/4/12	
Official Number. 131428					

Wages 6 days 14/-
Bonus 3. 0. 8
£3. 14. 8

WE, the undersigned, Members of the Crew of the above-named Ship, do hereby release the said Ship, and the Master and Owner or Owners thereof, from all claims for Wages or otherwise, in respect of the above named Voyage. And I, the Master, do hereby release the said undersigned Members of the Crew from all claims in respect of the said voyage.

Master.

NOTE.—Pursuant to Section 60 of the Merchant Shipping Act, 1906, there are excepted from this release the claims or demands which are specified on the back hereof, and which are identified by the signatures of the respective Seamen notifying such excepted claims or demands.

Dated the day of 19

Reference No. in Agreement.	Signatures of Crew.	Balance of Wages Paid.	Reference No. in Agreement.	Signatures of Crew.	Balance of Wages Paid.
	John Collins	3. 14. 8			

I attest the execution of the above Release in my presence subject to the exceptions above referred to (if any).

(Signed) (Signature of Official before whom Release was signed, with Official Seal.)

NOTE.—This form when completed should be forwarded at once to the Registrar General of Shipping and Seamen, London.

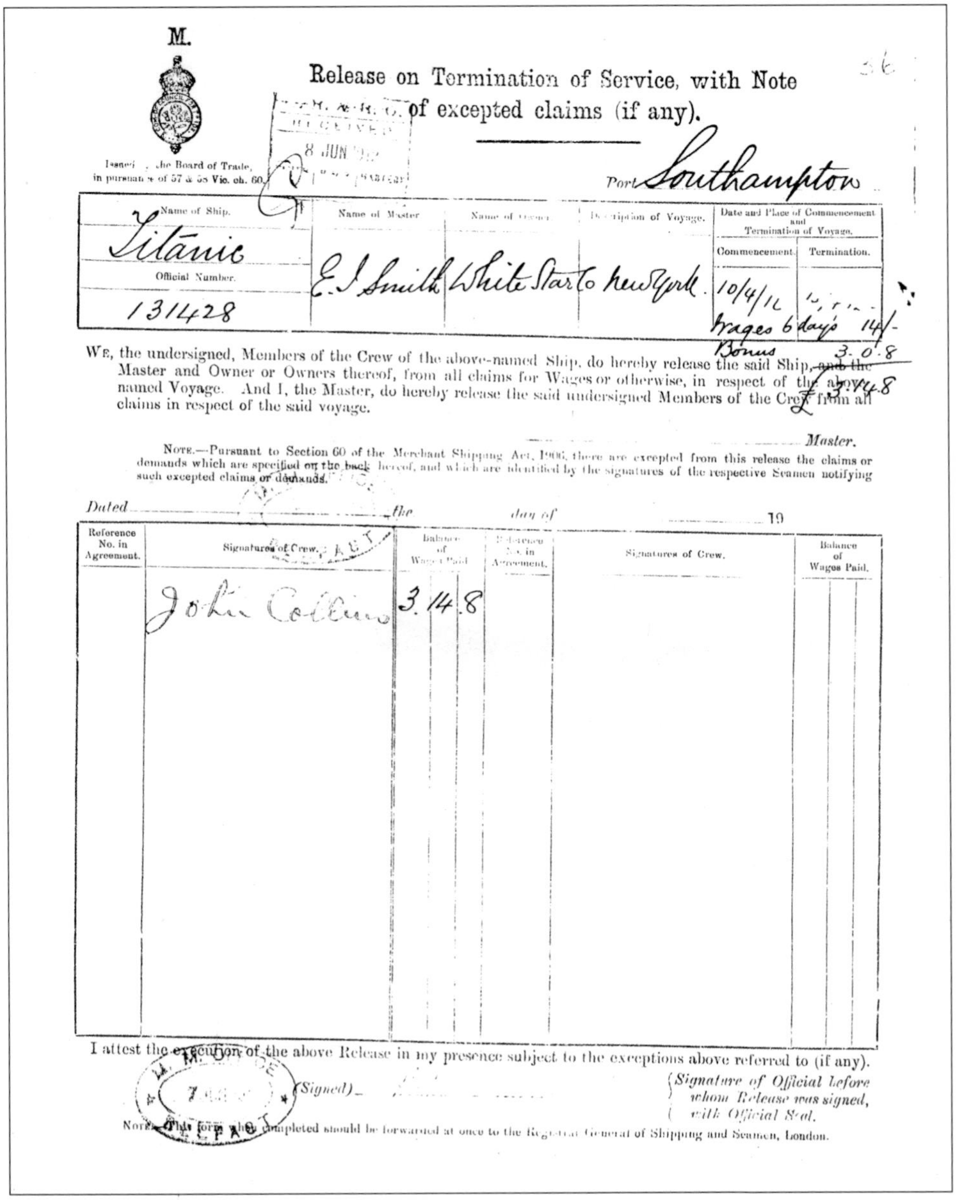

John Collins' discharge certificate.

(The National Archives, ref. BT100/259)

The child was washed out of John's grasp. When John surfaced, after what he felt was about two to three minutes, he was about four or five yards from an upturned lifeboat, the *Englehardt* (collapsible boat B). He swam towards it and climbed onto the keel. He received no help in climbing up; the fifteen or so people already there were watching the ship sinking. John said that when he looked at the *Titanic* he could see no visible lights, and that he heard the awful cries of people in the water.

At the American Inquiry, John said that all those who wanted a place on the *Englehardt* got one, except one poor soul. When this man swam up to the boat, John stated, he was told that he would overbalance the lifeboat if he got on board. The *Englehardt* was remaining afloat only because the people on her were keeping her balanced by moving their weight from side to side. This unknown swimmer said, 'That's all right, boys, keep cool, God bless you,' and swam away. John did not know what had happened to the swimmer, the two children, their mother or the steward who had been with him on the *Titanic*.[11]

John was formally discharged from the *Titanic* on 15 April 1912. He was paid six days' wages, which amounted to 14s., and a bonus of £3.0s.8d. By signing the discharge, John waived the right to pursue any claim against the White Star Line. After giving his evidence, he returned to the UK on the Red Star *Lapland*.

John died on 6 February 1941, at the age of forty-six.

Henry Philip Creese
(LOST) (pictured left — Institute of Marine Engineers)

Henry was born in 1868 in Falmouth, England. He was married and had two daughters, aged eight and fourteen. At the time of his death he had two addresses, one in Enfield Grove, Southampton, and one in the Stranmillis area of Belfast.

Henry was employed by the White Star Line as a deck engineer and was paid £10.10s. per month. He had served his apprenticeship at Harland and Wolff, and had then joined the Head Line Shipping Company; he had also served with the Ulster Steamship Company. In 1912, he had been with the White Star Line for about fourteen years, and had served on the *Olympic* before being transferred to the *Titanic*.

Henry joined the *Titanic* in Belfast, signing on on 2 April, and travelled with the ship to Southampton, where he signed on again on 6 April.

Alfred Flemming Cunningham
(LOST)

Alfred, who was employed by Harland and Wolff as an apprentice fitter, was a member of the guarantee group that sailed with the *Titanic*. He lived at

4 Spamount Street, Belfast, with his mother Elizabeth, his brothers James, Robert and Thomas, and his sisters Lilly and Martha.

On 20 April 1912, it was reported in the local press that Alfie, as his family called him, had survived the loss of the *Titanic*. Unfortunately, his family's joy was short-lived. On 26 April, the *Belfast Newsletter* broke the shattering news that Alfie had been lost. Harland and Wolff had received a telegram with the news that Alfred was not among the survivors. By this time it was known that all of the members of the guarantee group had been lost.

The terrible mix-up which gave Alfred's family false hope was caused by the fact that there was another A. Cunningham on board the *Titanic*. This second A. Cunningham (no relation to Alfred), who was employed as a bedroom steward, survived the disaster. He was later called to give evidence at the British Inquiry.

Alfred's brother, Robert, was also to lose his life at sea. He was Chief Officer on the *SS Castlebar*, and was lost at sea when the *Castlebar* sank on 13 March 1918.

Alfie's mother placed the following obituary in the local press in memory of her son:

> Hard and heavy was the stroke
> The cable brought across the sea,
> The death of one we love so well;
> His face on earth we'll never see.
> Not dead to me, I love him dear,
> Not lost but gone before,
> He lives with me in memory still
> and will for ever more.[12]

Thomas Patrick Dillon

(SURVIVED) (pictured right — *Daily Sketch*)

Thomas was employed by the White Star Line as a trimmer, and was paid £6 per month. When he signed on for the *Titanic*'s voyage, he gave his last address as 'Sailors' Home, Southampton'. Thomas was born in Liverpool, but lived in Belfast, and in 1912 he was thirty-four years old.

Thomas was the only Ulster member of the crew to be called to give evidence at the British Inquiry. He was asked a total of 270 questions, with 211 being asked by the Attorney General, Mr Raymond Asquith, and the Commissioner, Lord Mersey. He was paid £5.16s. in travelling and subsistence fees for his attendance.

At the inquiry, Thomas stated that he had helped to remove the coal from a bunker fire in the engine room, which had started in Belfast and continued to burn until twenty-four hours before the ship hit the iceberg. (This matter has raised questions as to how the extra heat generated by the fire might have affected the ship's hull.) When the *Titanic* collided with the iceberg, Thomas had been on duty in the engine room, engaged in cleaning duties; his boilers had not been lit at the time. He said that he had heard the telegraph ring, with the request that the engines be stopped. After that there had been an order for slow astern, for about two minutes. This was followed by an order for the engines to be set ahead for about another two minutes; then the signal had been given to stop.

The Chief Engineer then told Thomas to help another engineer to open the watertight bulkhead doors so that the rest of the engineers could go forward.

At about 1.15 a.m. on 15 April, according to Thomas, the order 'All hands on deck — put on your life-preservers,' was given. At this stage, he saw water coming into the engine-room from beneath the floor-plates, and he made his way to the well deck.

Thomas stated that he went down with the ship and sank about two fathoms. When he surfaced, he swam around for about twenty minutes before being picked up by the occupants of Lifeboat No. 4. After being picked up he saw about a thousand people in the water. He said that he had lost consciousness in the lifeboat; and that, on recovering, he had found Sailor Lyons and another unnamed sailor lying on top of him, dead.

Among the other people in Lifeboat No. 4 were Madeline Astor, wife of John Astor; Mrs Ryerson and her children; Mrs Thayer, Mrs Widner and Mrs Martha Stevenson. Mrs Stevenson later described Thomas's entry into the boat to Colonel Gracie, a first-class passenger who, in 1913, published *The Truth about the Titanic*, the first piece of in-depth research on the sinking.

> We pulled three men into the boat who had dropped off the ship and were swimming toward us. One man was drunk and had a bottle of brandy in his pocket which the quartermaster, W.J. Perkis, threw overboard. This drunk was thrown into the bottom of the boat and a blanket thrown over him.

It appears that 'this drunk' was Thomas, who had found the bottle of brandy on board the *Titanic* and — like any good Ulsterman — had done the right thing by it.

The story which Mrs Stevenson told Colonel Gracie is not the same as the one Thomas told Lord Mersey at the British Inquiry — Thomas's account of his rescue made no mention of the incident with the bottle!

Albert George Ervine
(LOST) (pictured left — Institute of Marine Engineers)
Albert was born in August 1893, and he lived with his parents on Old Cavehill Road, Belfast. He received his basic education in Belfast, and then, from 1907

to 1909, he attended evening classes in Practical Mathematics, Magnetism and Electricity at the Municipal Technical Institute in Belfast. Albert was very involved with the YMCA, and was a member of their Bible class. After the disaster, his Bible-class teacher, Mr D.A. Black, described 'Bertie' as having a frank disposition, a blameless life, and a winsome manner which had won the hearts of all who knew him.

Albert was employed by the White Star Line as an assistant electrician. His wages were £8 per month. He joined the *Titanic* in Belfast, signing the log on 2 April, for the trip to Southampton; on 6 April, he re-signed for the fateful journey.

After the *Titanic* sank, Albert's father received the following telegram from the White Star Line in Southampton: 'Deeply regret your son's name not in the list of those who were saved. Please accept our deepest sympathy.'[13]

Albert's death notice, printed in the *Belfast Newsletter* on 24 April 1912, contained the following verse:

> There is a Shepherd living there,
> The first-born from the dead,
> Who tends with sweet unwearied care
> The flock for which He bled.
> Oh earth, earth, earth,
> Hear the word of the Lord from the *Titanic*.
> Prepare to meet they God.[14]

Also on 24 April, a letter from Albert to his mother was published in a local paper.[15] The letter had been written on the *Titanic*, when she was about 80 miles from Queenstown, County Cork, and had been posted from there.

> Yours received in Cherbourg, France yesterday evening. We have had everything working nicely so far, except when leaving Southampton.
>
> As soon as the *Titanic* began to move out of the dock, the suction caused the *Oceanic*, which was alongside her berth, to swing outwards, while another liner the *New York*, broke loose altogether and bumped into the *Oceanic*. The gangway of the *Oceanic* simply dissolved.
>
> Middleton and myself were up top of the after funnel so we saw everything quite distinctly. I thought there was going to be a proper smash-up owing to the high wind, but I don't think that anyone was hurt.
>
> Well, we were over at Cherbourg last night. It was just a mass of fortifications. We are now on our way to County Cork. The next call then is New York.
>
> I am on duty morning and evening from 8 to 12 that is four hours' work and eight hours off. (Have just been away attending the alarm bell.)
>
> This morning we had a full dress rehearsal of an emergency. The alarm bells all rang for 10 seconds, then about 50 doors, all steel, gradually slid down into their places, so that water could not escape from any one section into the next.

So you see it would be impossible for the ship to be sunk in collision with another....

Alfred Middleton, was a twenty-six-year-old assistant engineer from County Sligo, and a close friend of Albert Ervine's. They had agreed to travel together. Alfred, like all the other engineers, died when the ship sank.

Hugh J. Fitzpatrick

(LOST) (pictured left — Institute of Marine Engineers)

Hugh was born in 1885, in Barrow, Furness, England. He lived at 171 Nelson Street, Belfast, with his wife Margaret. They had one child, who was born in 1911; and in April 1912, Margaret was expecting a second baby.

Hugh was employed by the White Star Line as an assistant boilermaker. He served his apprenticeship at Harland and Wolff, and joined White Star in 1905. He served as boilermaker on the *Baltic* and the *Romanic* before being transferred to the *Titanic*.

Hugh's journey with the *Titanic* began in Belfast. He joined the ship with the other engineers on 2 April, transferring from the *Romanic*, and then signed on again in Southampton on 6 April. His wages were £11 per month.

In June 1912, Margaret Fitzpatrick took Ismay, Imrie and Company to court at the Belfast Recorder's Court. Judge J. Walker Craig awarded her £100.

Anthony Wood Frost

(LOST) (pictured left — Patricia McDonald)

'Artie', as Anthony was known to friends and family, was born in Belfast in 1874. He was employed by Harland and Wolff as a foreman fitter, and sailed on the *Titanic* as part of the guarantee group. He and his wife, Lizzie Jane, had four children — one of whom, Marjorie, was the president of the former Ulster *Titanic* Society until her death in 1995.

The Frost family home was in Sunbury Avenue, Belfast. Artie joined Harland and Wolff as a machine-boy in January 1888, at the age of fourteen. The following year, he was appointed as an apprentice fitter. Once he had finished his apprenticeship, in March 1894, he left the shipyard and went to sea to gain experience. When he returned, two years later, he rejoined the shipyard. His standard of work and his energy singled him out for promotion to leading hand, in 1901. Artie's father, G.W. Frost, was a foreman fitter in the shipyard, and when he retired, in March 1907, Artie took over the job. At that time, his wages were £3.10s. per week, and over the next four years this was to increase to £4.5s. per week.

Artie supervised the fitting of the machinery on board both the *Olympic* and the *Titanic*. He was described as a most energetic and capable foreman, and there is little doubt that he was on the verge of further promotion.

It was reported that Artie was not in the engine room when the *Titanic* hit the iceberg. After the collision, he made his way down a steel access ladder to the engine room, which is where he was last seen.

The Harland and Wolff foreman's wages book for the week ending 2 May 1912 contains the entry, written in red ink beside the name A. Frost, 'Went down with *SS Titanic* 15/4/12' (illustration on page 13).

The directors of Harland and Wolff sent a letter of sympathy to the Frost family, and decided to continue to pay Artie's wages until July 1912. They also decided to donate up to £15 to pay for the education of the Frost children for a period of one year. If the school results obtained were satisfactory, this donation would be repeated.

George Cumming, a director of Harland and Wolff, sent the following letter to Artie's father George:

> Dear Mr Frost,
>
> It is with great pain that I write you regarding the sad bereavement which you and your family have suffered in the loss of your son, and my dear friend Artie.
>
> I think that you know perfectly well what I thought of him without my expressing it in a letter, but I may say, as I have done before, that he was always straightforward, and whenever there was any difficulty he was at his post.
>
> I feel sure you are very proud today that, although not saved, he was undoubtedly down below assisting the Staff in the Engine Room, and therefore met his death whilst doing his duty. Practically nothing has been said in the Press respecting the brave men below, who were really heroes.
>
> I sent him in the '*Titanic*' as he had not made a voyage in one of the large ships, and I hope you will accept my assurance that I considered at the time it was for his own good as well as the interests of the Firm. One of my aims was to promote him, as he had served us in a way which left nothing to be desired.
>
> Believe me, dear Mr Frost, that I feel deep sympathy for you and your family, also for his good wife and children, of whom he was so very proud, having often spoken to me about them.
>
> Yours sincerely,
>
> (Sgd.) Geo. Cumming.[16]

Artie's widow, Lizzie Jane, died in February 1961, within twenty-four hours of another *Titanic* widow — Susan Chisholm, the wife of Roderick Chisholm.

Years after the disaster, Artie's daughter Marjorie recalled the time of her father's death.[17] In 1912, she was four years old. She remembered that her mother cried a lot, and that their home always seemed to be crowded with people coming and going. She remembered hearing people remark 'Their father is lost,' and with the innocence of childhood, Marjorie and her sister Doreen went looking for him in Belfast, asking passers-by if they had seen their father.

Marjorie always spoke with great pride of Artie and the other gallant engineers who tried to save the *Titanic* on that fateful night which robbed her of her father. It is not surprising that she had a great fear of water.

In 1912, Mick Nolan, a family friend, wrote the following poem about Artie. It was sold as a single sheet, and proceeds went to the Lady Mayoress's Belfast Relief Fund.

ANTHONY FROST
(lost in the *Titanic* 1912)

by Mick Nolan

Sleep, hero, sleep in your watery grave,
Two miles below the ocean wave,
Free, comrade, free from care and pain,
But God hath said — we'll meet again.
We know the scripture which hath said
The sea shall yet give up its dead;
Though thy body lies near Labrador,
We'll meet one day on a brighter shore.
A nation hath been bathed in tears,
For the loss of the gallant engineers,
Though many dangers they had braved,
When the ship went down, not one was saved.
Like heroes true, these lads so brave,
At their post all met a watery grave;
You have left a wife and children dear,
Who are proud of their gallant engineer.
They, with your father — old and grey,
Will meet you on the Judgement Day;
When God above will say — my son,
Come unto Me, it is well done.[18]

Thomas Graham
(SURVIVED)

Thomas was born in 1884 and lived at 28 Downpatrick Street, Belfast. He was employed by the White Star Line as a fireman.

He signed on for the run to Southampton on 29 March 1912, with instructions to report for duty on 1 April at 4.00 a.m. He sailed from Belfast on the *Titanic* on 2 April. On 6 April, he signed on for the voyage to New York. He survived the sinking, and was officially discharged from the *Titanic* on 15 April 1912. On his discharge he was paid £3.16s., which was made up of his monthly wage of £1.4s. and a bonus of £2.12s. Like the other surviving members of the crew, he signed away any right to make a claim against the White Star Line, and his wages were stopped from the moment the ship sank.

Thomas was later called to the British Inquiry, but was not called as a witness, although he was paid £7.15s. for expenses.

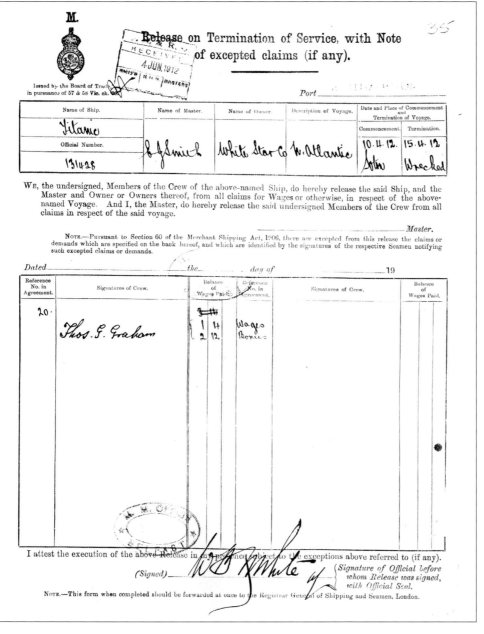

Thomas Graham's discharge certificate.

(The National Archives, ref. BT100/259)

John Haggan
(SURVIVED)

John — or Johnny, as he was known to family and friends — was born in 1877 in Belfast, the first of Edward and Mary Haggan's eight children. He never married, and he lived at the family home, 49 Thorndyke Street, Belfast.

At the age of twenty, he joined the Royal Horse Artillery. He served in the Boer War, and in 1901 was in the parade at Queen Victoria's funeral. He then joined the White Star Line as a fireman, at a wage of £6 per month. Before signing on for the *Titanic*, he served on the *Brayhead*. His first contact with the *Titanic* was when he signed on in Belfast on 29 March 1912, with instructions to report for duty on 1 April at 4.00 a.m. On 6 April 1912, in Southampton, John signed on for the *Titanic*'s voyage to New York.

John later recalled the events of 14 April in a letter to Colonel Gracie, which Gracie referred to in his account of the sinking.[19]

John said that Lightoller told him to assist in releasing the *Englehardt*, Lifeboat B, from the top of the officers' quarters. At this stage, the *Titanic*'s bows would have been underwater. John cut the rope holding the lifeboat's oars, and was passing an oar down to a crew member when the lifeboat floated into the water. John jumped down to the boat deck and then into the water, and clung to the keel of the overturned boat. He said that he felt he was staring death in the face. One of the funnels started to fall; it missed John and the boat by about a yard, and the splash it created pushed them about thirty yards from the ship. John managed to climb onto the keel of the lifeboat, where he and fourteen other people — including Second Officer Lightoller and Colonel Gracie — succeeded in standing up and, by delicate balancing under Lightoller's instructions, remained afloat.

One swimmer who approached them was turned away, as they feared his additional weight would swamp the boat. The swimmer bade them all farewell; before he swam away he asked for a plank to hold on to, but he was told to cling to whatever he could. John said that it was very hard to see such a brave man swim away, and that he would never forget the cries of distress of the people in the water.

Someone on the boat asked the religion of those present and found a mixture of Presbyterians, Roman Catholics and Episcopalians. Someone suggested that they say the Lord's Prayer, and this met with everyone's approval.

John and the others on the overturned boat were eventually transferred to Boat 12, where at least they were able to sit down. They were finally rescued by the *Carpathia*.

John's father, Edward, received a telegram stating that he had been saved, and John travelled home in the Red Star *Lapland*.

John died on 13 January 1952, at the age of seventy-five, in the Royal Victoria Hospital, Belfast.

Pastor John Harper

(LOST) (pictured right — Harper Memorial Baptist Church)

Although Pastor John Harper was not born in Ulster, he did have an Ulster connection, being well known in Belfast, especially in East Belfast.

John was born in Renfrewshire, Scotland, in May 1872. He came from a devout Christian family, so it was no surprise when he received the call to the ministry. He was the first minister of Paisley Road Baptist Church, in Kinniny Park, Glasgow. He married, but his wife died in childbirth in 1906. However, their daughter, Nina, survived.

John preached throughout the United Kingdom, but it was his preaching at an evangelistic Mission at the Mountpottinger Baptist Tabernacle, Templemore Avenue, Belfast, that made him very well known throughout the city.

He was travelling on the *Titanic* with his daughter, Nina, who was then six years old, and his niece Jessie Leitch. Their destination was the Moody Church in Chicago.

In May 1972, the Harper Memorial Baptist Church produced a booklet entitled 'Sent From God'. It describes how, the night before the *Titanic* sank, John Harper was seen

> ... earnestly seeking to lead a young man to living faith in Christ. Afterwards, when on the ship's deck, [Harper] commented on a glint of red in the sky towards the west. His recorded words were, 'It will be beautiful in the morning.' It certainly was a glorious dawn for John Harper. He saw the beauty of Christ whom he loved and served so well.[20]

A passenger from Ontario, Canada, who survived the sinking, later recalled that, as he was clinging to a piece of wood, he saw John Harper in the water. John called out to him, 'Man, are you saved?' The man replied, 'No, I am not.' John advised this man to attend to his soul, and not much later, asked him, 'Are you saved yet?' John then slipped below the waves. This man claims to be John's last convert.

Nina Harper and Jessie Leitch were placed in a lifeboat and survived. Years later, in December 1921, Nina performed the opening ceremony of the Harper Memorial Baptist Church, in Glasgow, which is dedicated to John's memory.

While he was on board the *Titanic*, John wrote the following letter to his friend Charles Livingstone and posted it from Queenstown. The two men had met in Scotland in 1895, when Livingstone heard Harper preach at an open-air evangelistic service. They had formed a lifelong friendship, and Harper had encouraged Livingstone to start a Mission that was to become the Paisley Road Baptist Mission.

The letter was posted in Queenstown. It is dated 11 April 1912.

> My dear Brother Livingstone,
>
> I am penning this little note just before we sail into Queenstown. Thus far the passage is all that can be desired. Nan and Jessie are with me and both doing well. We sailed from Southampton to Cherbourg in France and thence to Queenstown and then on to New York. We had a glorious time in the past few days in Falworth, a real breath of revival. Oh that it may continue and spread.[21]

Herbert Gifford Harvey

(LOST) (pictured left — Institute of Marine Engineers)

Herbert was born in Belfast on 3 February 1878. He was the fourth son of J. Thompson Harvey, of the well-known Belfast firm of Lawther and Harvey. He was employed by the White Star Line as an assistant second engineer, and his pay in 1912 was £12.10s. per month. He had two addresses, one at 211 Belmont Road, Belfast; and the other at Obelisk Road in Southampton. He was engaged to be married, and was in the Masonic Order.

Herbert was educated at Portora Royal School, Enniskillen, and served his apprenticeship at the Belfast and Northern Counties Railway at York Street, Belfast. He then volunteered to serve with the 46th Company Imperial Yeomanry in South Africa, and was awarded the King's Medal with one clasp and the Queen's Medal with three clasps. He also worked for Harland and Wolff and for the Nitrate Producers Steamship Company. He then joined the White Star Line, serving on the *Teutonic* and the *Olympic* before being transferred to the *Titanic*. He signed on, in Belfast, for the *Titanic*'s voyage to Southampton on 2 April, with the other engineers. On 6 April, in Southampton, he signed on for the trip to New York.

At the time of the collision, Herbert and two other engineers, Bertie Wilson and Jonathan Shepherd, were on duty in the engine room. Also on duty were eighty-four men — fifty-four stokers, twenty-four coal trimmers and six leading firemen. Herbert took control and ordered the stokers to remove the fires from the boilers, so as to allow the boilers to cool. The lights

114

in the engine room went out, and Herbert sent Barrett, a fireman, to fetch some lamps; before Barrett returned, however, the lights had come back on again. Herbert also gave the stokers the command to leave the engine room. Before this, however, he had a floor plate lifted, so that he could gain access to floor valves; Jonathan Shepherd fell into this unguarded opening, breaking his leg.

Herbert was last seen in the engine room.

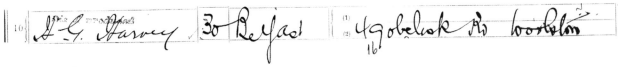

James Heslim
(LOST)

James was born in Cork, Ireland, in 1867. He was employed by the White Star Line as a trimmer, and in 1912 his wage was £5.10s. per month.

He married Brigid (Biddy) Burns, who was a native of Jonesborough, County Armagh, and they set up house in Edenappa, Jonesborough. James and Biddy had two children, May and Thomas.

James transferred from the *Olympic* to her sister ship, the *Titanic*, joining her at Southampton, where he signed on on 6 April.

Biddy died in 1967 in a nursing home in Newry, at the grand old age of a hundred and five; she was the oldest widow of the *Titanic*. Her daughter, May, spent the last years of her life in the same nursing home as her mother, and died at the age of eighty-six, more than three-quarters of a century after the disaster.

All her life, Biddy loved to sing 'If I Were a Blackbird'. James used to sing it to her, and it was one of the last things he sang before he left on the *Titanic*.

> If I Were a Blackbird
>
> If I were a blackbird I'd whistle and sing
> and I'd follow the ship that my true love sails in
> and on the top rigging I'd there build my nest
> and I'd pillow my head on his lily-white breast.[22]

Robert Hopkins
(SURVIVED)

Robert was born in 1872. He was employed by the White Star Line as an able seaman, and his pay in 1912 was £5 per month.

On 2 April 1912, he sailed with the *Titanic* from Belfast to Southampton, on ticket No. 205; he had signed on in Belfast on 29 March, with instructions to report for duty on 1 April. On reaching Southampton, he again signed the ship's log. He was one of the very few crew members who entered their last recorded ship as '*Titanic*' on the Southampton log; not even the senior officers did this.

Robert survived the sinking, and was discharged from the White Star Line. Records list his service as terminating on 15 April 1912 'at sea'. He was paid wages amounting to £3.0s.4d.

He gave his Belfast address as 4 Woodstock Road, which in 1912, was a pub called the Primrose Bar. The area has since been demolished and rebuilt.

Robert Knight
(LOST)

Robert was employed by Harland and Wolff as a leading hand fitter. He lived at 21 Yarrow Street, Belfast, with his wife and four children. He was a member of the Masonic Order attached to the Hertford Lodge.

He started work at the shipyard on 2 June 1891, and worked there for twenty-one years. He was valued as a steady worker, and on 1 January 1903 he was promoted to a leading hand fitter. It was believed that his energy and attention to his work would have brought him further promotion.

Matthew Leonard
(LOST) (pictured left — *Belfast Telegraph*)

Matthew Leonard was born in 1886, and lived at 45 Chatwell Street, Belfast, with his widowed mother and his sister.

Matthew signed on for the *Titanic*'s voyage on 4 April 1912; his entry in the log gives his place of birth as 'United States of America'. Like the *Titanic*, Matthew was on his maiden voyage: it was the first time he had gone to sea to earn a living. He was employed by the White Star Line as a steward, at a wage of £3.15s. per month. His previous employers had been the well-known Belfast jewellers, Joseph Rea's of Ann Street, who are still in business at the time of publication.

James McGrady
(LOST) (pictured right — Allison Murphy)

James came from County Down. He was born around 1896 in Lisnamore, Crossgar. His father, James McGrady, was a railway worker who married a local girl, Ann Higgins. Young James, who was called Hugh by his family, never knew his father, who died before James was born; his mother remarried a local farmer, Tom Savage.

As a child, James was walking home from school one day, along the railway tracks, when he noticed a loose sleeper. He ran to Crossgar Railway Station and managed to stop a train before it left, probably saving numerous lives. The railway company gave him a free pass for life on the Belfast and County Down Railway.

At the age of sixteen, James decided to go to sea and joined the White Star Line as a fireman; he was paid £3.15s. per month. He joined the *Titanic* on 6 April in Southampton, transferring from the *Oceanic*.

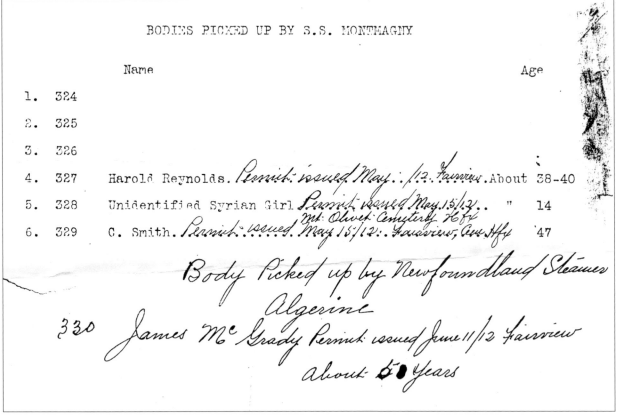

Above: Record of Body No. 330. (PRO Halifax)

118

James's unfortunate claim to fame is that his body was the last to be recovered from the North Atlantic; it was found sometime around 25 May 1912, by the *SS Montmagny*. His body is listed as No. 330 to be recovered. A permit for burial was issued on 11 June 1912, and the interment took place at Fairview Cemetery, Halifax.

James was wearing a lifebelt when his body was found, and this is reputed to be the same one that is on display in a Newfoundland museum.

Grave marker for James McGrady's burial place in Fairview Cemetery, Halifax, Canada.
(Author's collection)

William McQuillan
(LOST) (pictured left — Marjorie Wilson)

William was born in 1886, the youngest son of William and Annie McQuillan. He had two sisters, Annie and Harriet, and lived at 79 Seaview Street, Belfast. He and his wife Margaret had two children.

William was employed by the White Star Line as a fireman, at a wage of £6 per month. He was discharged from the *Highland Glen* before signing on to the *Titanic* on 29 March 1912. He had to report for duty on the *Titanic* by 4.00 a.m. on 1 April, to prepare for the sea trials and the trip to Southampton. On arrival at Southampton, he re-signed for the next leg of the journey. His instructions were to be on the ship on sailing day, 10 April, no later than 6.00 a.m.

His body was recovered by the *Mackay-Bennett* and identified as body No. 183. The following is the recorded description of the body:

BODY No. 183
MALE

Hardly any hair on head or face.
CLOTHING: Blue coat and vest, dungaree pants, striped shirt.
EFFECTS: Shaving brush, soap, papers, National Fireman's Union Book Number 932.[23]

A permit for burial was issued on 6 May 1912, and the body was interred at Fairview Cemetery, Halifax.

William's widow, Margaret, took Ismay, Imrie and Company to court at the Belfast Recorder's Court on 23 June 1912, requesting arbitration and apportionment. She was represented by Mr T.J. Campbell. Judge J. Walker Craig, before making an award for compensation, commented on how young the men who had been lost on the *Titanic* were. Margaret and her children were each awarded £79.12s.

William McReynolds

(LOST) (pictured right — Institute of Marine Engineers)

William, known to his family and friends as Willie, was born in 1890. He was single and lived with his parents and his sister, Maggie, at Lagan Villas, Belfast. Willie was a member of the Lodge Temperance Dart Club.

When Willie left school, he was apprenticed to Harland and Wolff's Engineering Department. He joined the White Star Line in March 1912. His journey on the *Titanic* was his first sea voyage. He was employed by the shipping line as the sixth engineer, and his pay was £8.10s. per month.

Willie joined the *Titanic* in Belfast on 2 April 1912, with the other engineers. On 6 April, in Southampton, he signed on again for the maiden voyage.

Thomas Millar

(LOST) (pictured right — Rupert Millar)

Thomas was born in Carrickfergus, County Antrim, in 1882. He lived at Meadow-brook Street, Belfast. He was employed by the White Star Line as an assistant deck engineer, at a wage of £9.10s. per month.

Having served his apprenticeship at Harland and Wolff, Thomas then worked at Vickers Limited of Barrow for a year, and at the shipyard of Workman Clark and Company of Belfast (known as 'the wee yard') for six months. He then returned to Harland and Wolff, where he worked for eight years before joining the White Star Line. He sailed on the *Gothland* before transferring to the *Titanic* — the fatal journey was only his second sea voyage. It is interesting to note that Thomas not only worked on the *Titanic*'s construction in the shipyard, but also sailed on her as a crew member.

Thomas's main reason for joining the *Titanic* was to sail to New York and find a new home in America. His wife, Jeannie, had died a few months before, and Thomas had left their two sons, Ruddick and Tommy, in the care of an aunt. He planned to send for them when he had found a home in America.

Thomas signed on the *Titanic* on 29 March, in Belfast. On arrival in Southampton he signed on for the fateful voyage.

Before Thomas sailed on the *Titanic*, he gave his eldest son, Ruddick, two new 1912 pennies. Thomas's grandson, Rupert Millar, remembers what his father said about these pennies and about Thomas's death:

> Rummaging through a drawer one evening, I came upon a little box with two pennies in it. The date on them was 1912, but they still looked brand-new. The find took my memory back to the time when I was a boy of four and my father pressed the coins into my hand before he went on a long journey. 'They're this year's,' Thomas said. 'Don't spend them until I get back.' Well, I haven't, and I never will.
>
> When the *Titanic* had gone, my brother Tommy and I went to stay with our aunt at a little village called Boneybefore, on the shore of Belfast Lough.

119

I liked it there, mainly because there was a stream where I could sail my paper boats. It was there that my cousin Maud found me one day. She looked worried and uneasy. I was watching one of my paper boats going serenely downstream, and just as she reached me, my frail boat hit a stone, quivered for a moment and then sank below the water.

'So your wee boat's sunk,' said Maud.

'Yes,' I said. 'But Tommy, my brother, will make another.'

'You remember that big boat that your da went on?' asked Maud.

'Uh-huh,' I said.

'Well,' said Maud, 'it was just like your wee boat. It hit an iceberg. A lot of people were drowned. Your da was drowned too.'

I stared at Maud blankly. Drowned? Did that mean that he was dead — that he would never come back?

My first thoughts were of his gold watch and chain, a magnificent affair that had always fascinated me. If he'd been lost, was the watch lost as well? Young people can sometimes be cruelly frank. Was it an avaricious streak in my make-up showing itself? Or was it that my youthful mind could not grasp immediately the awful fact that my father would not come back again — that in future years he would merely be a name on a memorial in front of Belfast's City Hall?

I cried bitterly and clutched my two pennies.[24]

In a Carrickfergus cemetery is a gravestone with the inscription:

In Loving Memory of
Our Dear Mother
Jeannie Millar
Who died on 18th Jan. 1912
Also our Dear Father
Thomas Millar
Lost in the *Titanic* Disaster 15th April 1912
'Until the Day Break'

Thomas Rowan Morrow
(LOST)

Thomas — or Tommy, as his family called him — was born in 1882 in Rathfriland, County Down; he had a brother, Robert (Robbie), and a sister, Mary. Tommy himself was a farmer at Drumlough. He was a prominent Orangeman, and had been Worshipful Master of his local Lodge for many years.

Tommy and a longtime friend, Robert, travelled from Rathfriland to Queenstown to board the *Titanic*. For some unrecorded reason, Robert was unable to get a place in the tender that was to transport them out to the *Titanic*, which was moored in the bay. Tommy did get a place, and sailed on the *Titanic* as a third-class passenger. He was lost. Robert, his friend, later travelled to America on the *Lusitania*.

William Murdoch
(SAVED)

William — who had the same name as the First Officer of the *Titanic* — was employed by the White Star Line as a fireman, and in 1912 his pay was £6 per month. He lived at 78 Thorndyke Street, Belfast, with his wife, Catherine. They had three children — Ann Martin, William John and Joseph.

William joined the *Titanic* in Belfast on 1 April, at 4.00 a.m., after signing on on 29 March with the other firemen. He travelled to Southampton and re-signed on 6 April for the next leg of the journey. He was discharged from the ship on 15 April; the logbook records the place of discharge as Latitude 41.16N, Longitude 50.14W — the North Atlantic. He was given £1.4s. which he was owed in wages. After the disaster, William was called as a witness by the British Inquiry, and was paid £8.05 for expenses.

On his return to Belfast, William described his lucky escape to the local press. He stated that at about 11.35 p.m. on 14 April, as he was preparing to go on duty, the *Titanic* struck the iceberg. He said that there was a dull grating noise, which did not cause any concern amongst the passengers or crew. He reported for duty at the stokehold, and soon found that the ship was taking on water. The firemen all remained on duty at their posts until midnight, when Chief Officer Bell instructed them to go on deck and put on lifejackets. The engineers, William said, all remained at their posts until the end.

William was directed to Lifeboat No. 16, but before boarding the boat he returned to his quarters to get extra warm clothing. When he came back on deck, he helped people into one of the collapsible lifeboats. He then assisted with the lowering of boat No.16, which he said held about forty-five people. At this stage, he said, the scene was heart-rending — some people were jumping into the water, and others were refusing to leave loved ones behind.

William helped to lower one of the collapsible lifeboats and then jumped into the water himself, coming up beside the collapsible, into which he climbed. (This would appear to be Collapsible D, which also held the noted Molly Brown and the two kidnapped Navratil children.) They rowed the lifeboat about a hundred yards from the *Titanic*. Then, William said, the *Titanic*'s bow started to slip underwater, while her stern projected out of the water, and her lights went out. William said that she remained in that position for two or three minutes before gliding below the

William Murdoch in Australia with Catherine Robson.

(Maureen Howard)

water, almost as quietly as she had left the slip on her launch day.

William was quite certain that he heard the band playing what he described as 'that well-known hymn', 'Nearer My God to Thee', just before the bow slipped below the water. He also said that it was a bitterly cold night. He only saw a few people in the water, but he felt that it was so cold that no one could endure it for long. He said that they were in the lifeboat for about six hours before being rescued by the *Carpathia*. Finally, he stated that it was absolutely untrue that Captain Smith committed suicide.

William emigrated to Australia in the mid-1920s, and continued to work on the sea, sailing on coastal ships between Sydney and Newcastle, Australia, for many years.

He often told the story of his escape from the *Titanic* to his children and grandchildren, recalling how, after the ship went down, he found a small child in the water, alive. They later found the child's mother, but she had lost the rest of her family.

William passed away in 1941. One of his grandchildren, Maureen Howard, remembers her grandfather as a wonderful man who was loved by all.

Francis (Frank) Parkes
(LOST) (pictured left — J. Lyons)

Frank, as his family and friends called him, was employed by Harland and Wolff as an apprentice plumber, and travelled on the *Titanic* as part of the guarantee group. He lived at 25 Agincourt Street, Belfast, with his parents. His father, Francis, was an official with the Belfast City Council, where he rose to the position of deputy town clerk. Frank had four brothers — Matthew, Robert George, Frederick, and Charles, who also worked at the Harland and Wolff shipyard. He also had two sisters — Lily, who married Thomas Henderson, and Violet Maud, who emigrated to the United States of America.

William Henry Marsh Parr
(LOST)

William was born in 1882 in Horwich, Lancashire, England. He served his apprenticeship in the Electrical Department of the Lancashire and Yorkshire Railway, finishing early in 1910. Later that year, he entered the service of Harland and Wolff as an assistant manager in the Electrical Department, fitting out ships. He supervised the electrical installations on both the *Olympic* and the *Titanic*. Harland and Wolff showed their confidence in him by selecting him as a member of the guarantee group.

William lived with his wife and young child at 16 Elaine Street, Belfast. He belonged to University Road Methodist Church, and was a devoted and respected teacher in their Sunday school.

A photograph — taken on board the *Titanic*, before she reached Queenstown, by Frank (later Father) Browne — shows William in the background, sitting on a mechanical camel, dressed in a long overcoat and flat cap. In the foreground is Mr T.W. Cawley, the ship's fitness instructor. In the original album of *Titanic* photographs, Father Browne mentions William as 'Mr Parr, Electrician'. The image of him is blurred.

On 28 April 1912, a letter from William's mother, who lived in Cheshire, was read to his Sunday school class. Mrs Parr mentioned William's strong attachment to the Sunday school and to his class of boys. She also pointed out that William remained faithfully at his post as an electrician right up to the last minute, helping to keep the lights on. She concluded her letter by echoing her husband's desire that all members of their son's class might become faithful servants of Christ.

Archibald Scott
(LOST)

Archibald was born in 1872. He was employed by the White Star Line as a fireman, at a wage of £6 per month. He lived at 262 Conway Street, Belfast, with his wife, Martha.

He joined the *Titanic* in Southampton, transferring from the *Oceanic* and signing on with the other firemen on 6 April. His wife was awarded £237.12s. in a case taken against Ismay, Imrie and Company Ltd.

Wilfred Seward
(SAVED)

Wilfred, who was born in 1887, was the chief pantryman (second class) on the *Titanic*. He was a Londoner, and when he joined the ship, he gave his address as 54 Stamford Street, London.

In 1954 he moved to Ballymoney, County Antrim. In 1962, to mark the fiftieth anniversary of the sinking, the *Constitution* newspaper carried a full account of Wilfred's time on the *Titanic*.

In the article, he stated that he joined the ship in Belfast (this would have been between 26 March and 2 April), but did not sign the Articles of Agreement. He said that when the *Titanic* struck the iceberg, he was off duty and was lying on his bunk. He continued:

> I remember one of my staff coming to the cabin and telling me that the ship had bumped something. I didn't think it was anything important so I just lay

on my bunk, and read on. Shortly afterwards, someone called, 'You'd better get up, there's something wrong.' I went on deck and was told we had hit an iceberg. I was ordered into a boat; there were about fifty or sixty other people with me. When we were being lowered and still a long way above the water, the boat capsized and we were all pitched into the water.

He went on to recall that the water was freezing cold and that his whole body was numb. He continued:

There was ice everywhere. It was some time before I was picked up. The lifeboat that I was in was about a hundred yards from the *Titanic*. I did not realise that there was anything seriously wrong until I saw the distress rockets go up, and then it registered. As she went down I heard terrible screams, like people yelling wildly at a football match, and then there was nothing but silence.[25]

Wilfred, like the other survivors, was picked up by the *Carpathia* and taken to New York.

Following his rescue, Wilfred was called to give evidence at the British Inquiry. He received expenses of £10.8s. He was called on the fifteenth day of the Inquiry, and was asked forty-four questions. During his questioning he did not mention that the lifeboat had capsized. He also stated that when he arrived on deck, he helped several passengers on with their life-jackets. He said that he first made his way to Boat No. 5 but then went to his allocated boat, No. 3; among the other survivors on board were Mrs Spedden and her son Douglas.

A very different account of the launch of Boat No. 3 was given by Miss Elizabeth W. Shutes. She stated that, while the lifeboat was being lowered down the side of the *Titanic*, rough seamen were all giving different orders; there was no officer on board, and the ropes lowering the boat were only working on one side. She stated that at one time the lifeboat was in such a position that it seemed it must capsize in mid-air. Miss Shutes added that the ropes finally began to work, and that the boat entered the water safely and pulled away from the *Titanic*.

This report totally contradicts the story that Wilfred told in the newspaper article; and, as previously stated, at the British Inquiry, he made no mention of the lifeboat capsizing into the water.

His story does, however, answer another riddle in the *Titanic* story. The *Titanic* sailed from Belfast at around 8.00 p.m. on 2 April 1912, and arrived at Southampton in the first few minutes of 4 April — the 570-mile journey having lasted approximately twenty-eight hours. The crew would have required a full day's meals during the sea trials on 2 April, followed by breakfast, lunch, dinner and supper on 3 April. However, although the crew that took the *Titanic* from Belfast to Southampton is clearly listed in the Articles of Agreement signed in Belfast before 2 April, no galley crew members appear on the log. So how were the crew fed over this period?

We know that Wilfred and Charles Joughin, the chief baker, joined the *Titanic* in Belfast. For some reason, however, neither Wilfred nor Charles — nor the other members of the galley staff who would be required to cater for the crew — signed the Articles of Agreement.

John Edward Simpson MB BCh BAO
(LOST) (pictured right — Kate Dornan)

John was employed by the White Star Line as an assistant surgeon. His father, John, was also a doctor. John Jr was born in 1875 and was the only boy in the family; he had five sisters, Lizelle, Caroline, Charlotte, Flora and Winifred. The family home was in Pakenham Place, Belfast.

John studied at the Royal Belfast Academical Institute and at the Royal University of Ireland, and took his medical degree at Queen's University, Belfast. His Belfast address was the family home in Pakenham Place; he also had accommodation at The Old Chestnuts, Tottenham Road, Hornsbury.

In 1905, John met, and married, Annie Edith Peters of Astley, Lancashire. They had one son, John Ralph Peters Simpson, who died in London on 25 March 1961.

John, a Lieutenant with the 1st Volunteer Battalion of the Duke of Cambridge's Own (Middlesex Regiment), until the disbandment of the Volunteers, was also a captain in the Royal Army Medical Corps, a member of the Ulster Association in London, and Vice-President of the Hornsey Branch of the Tariff Reform League.

John took to the sea because his health was deteriorating and it was felt that a few sea voyages would be beneficial to him. For some years, he served as the Medical Officer with the Peninsular and Oriental Steamship Company. He then joined the White Star Line and served as the assistant surgeon on the *Olympic*. He was transferred to the *Titanic* in Southampton. The senior surgeon on the *Titanic*, Dr O'Loughlin, had joined the ship in Belfast, and sailed with her to Southampton. John signed the log for the *Titanic* on 6 April 1912. As assistant surgeon, he was responsible for the second- and third-class passengers.

On 11 April 1912, while the *Titanic* was approaching Queenstown, John wrote a letter to his mother in Belfast; the letter was posted to her from Queenstown. In the letter, John told his mother that he had travelled from Liverpool and boarded the *Titanic* at 10.00 a.m. on 6 April. He continued:

> I am very well and am gradually getting settled in my new cabin which is larger than my last .... I found my two trunks unlocked and 5 or 6 dollars stolen out of my pocketbook. I hope none of my stamps have been stolen.[26]

On board R·M·S·"TITANIC".

11th April 1912

Dear Mother,

I travelled from Liverpool on Monday by the 12 o'c train & arrived on board at 10 p.m. feeling pretty tired. I am very well & am gradually getting settled in my new cabin which is larger than my last. This pleases all the time as if it were the Olympic & I like it very much. I am a member of the Club now which is an advantage. Be sure to let me know how

Letter written by John Simpson to his mother. (Kate Dornan)

He finished the letter — which bears the White Star flag and the words 'On board the R.M.S. TITANIC' — with the words 'With fondest love, John'.

After the disaster, a close friend of John's, a Mr R. Graham, wrote to Second Officer Charles Lightoller — who was the senior surviving officer of the *Titanic* — for information about John's fate. Lightoller replied with the following letter, which was written on board the *SS Adriatic*, on 1 May 1912:

128

Dear Sir,

In reply to yours of 30th ult. I am sorry to say that Assistant Surgeon John E. Simpson was on the *Titanic*. I deeply regret your loss, which is also mine. I may say I was practically the last man to speak to Dr. Simpson, and on this occasion he was walking along the boat deck in company with Messrs McElroy and Barker, Dr O'Loughlin, and four assistant pursers. They were all perfectly calm, in the knowledge that they had done their duty, and were still assisting by showing a calm and cool exterior to the passengers. Each one individually came up to me and shook hands. We merely exchanged the words 'good-bye, old man!' This occurred shortly before the end, and I am not aware that he was seen by anyone after. With deepest sympathy for you in the loss of your friend, believe me,

Yours Sincerely

C.H. Lightoller[27]

On 7 May 1912, Mr Graham wrote to John's father, Doctor Edward Simpson. He told him of Lightoller's letter, and referred to John as a 'warm friend'. The letter concluded:

We had had only a few too-short visits from John but I had come to look forward to them for his hearty good fellowship, and my good wife and my girls all have a share in your sorrow.

With deepest sympathy to Mrs Simpson and yourself.

Yours sincerely

R.W. Graham[28]

After this, Dr Simpson wrote to Charles Lightoller, enclosing some photographs of John. Lightoller replied on 6 June 1912, thanking the doctor for the photographs. In his letter, Lightoller comments:

Very many thanks for the photos of your son, which believe me I prize very much .... I think the one without his beard is a more excellent likeness of him, as I knew him.[29]

He signed the letter 'Yours very sincerely, C.H. Lightoller'.

Later in 1912, John's sister Lizelle travelled to Australia on board the *SS Medic* to see her sister Flora. On 8 October 1912, she wrote to her mother from Melbourne:

I came round by the '*Medic*' and saw Mr Lowe [Harold Lowe had been the Fifth Officer on board the *Titanic*, and had survived the sinking] after I got on board. He was speaking to Jack [John] after the collision. It was dark and he could not see very well when getting a boat lowered. Jack came to him and said — 'here is something that will be useful to you', bringing him an electric torch.

He never saw him after that.

Mr Lowe was in bed with a broken leg so I did not see him again until we got in port.[30]

Lizelle tells her mother how she and Flora visited Harold Lowe, bringing him flowers and fruit, and continues:

It is very dull for him as he is not allowed to get up at all. I told him that Father would be very glad to see him if he ever went to Belfast and asked him to call.

She signs the letter, 'Much love to all, Your loving daughter Lizelle Simpson'.

In the quiet setting of Bangor Abbey Churchyard is a headstone commemorating John and several of his relatives. The inscription, which is almost a family history, reads:

To be with Christ which is far better
In loving memory of Charlotte third daughter of John Simpson,
M.D. Belfast, who died 29th November 1890 aged 13 years.
His only son John Edward Ship's Surgeon, *Titanic*,
Lost 15th April 1912, aged 37 years.
Also his grandchild, son of Robert and Winifred Stanton,
16th June 1918
Also his fourth daughter Flora died 8th June 1920
Also his daughter Lizette died 8th February 1948
Also his grandson John Ralph Peters,
died in London 25th March 1961,
son of the above John Edward.

The Royal Belfast Academical Institute erected a brass plaque in their Common Hall in memory of both John and another alumnus who was lost with the *Titanic*, Thomas Andrews. The plaque was unveiled on 28 April 1913.

TO THE MEMORY OF
THOMAS ANDREWS JUNIOR,
AND JOHN EDWARD SIMPSON M.B.
WHO ON THE NIGHT OF THE 14th APRIL 1912
WENT DOWN IN MID-OCEAN WITH THE SS TITANIC
GIVING THEIR LIVES THAT OTHERS MIGHT BE SAVED.
THIS TABLET HAS BEEN ERECTED BY THE
BELFAST OLD INSTONIANS ASSOCIATION

'FORTUNATI AMBO NULLA DIES UNQUAM
MEMORI VOS EXIMET AEVO'

Mary Sloan
(SURVIVED) (pictured right — *Belfast Telegraph*)

Mary was born in Ulster in 1884. She lived at Kerrsland Terrace, Belfast, with her mother, and had two sisters. Mary was employed by the White Star Line as a stewardess, at a wage of 16s. per week. After the disaster, she was called to the British Inquiry and paid £8.12s.6d. for expenses, but was not called to give evidence.

Mary was well known to travellers on the Belfast–Liverpool channel crossing, as she had been a stewardess on the *SS Magic*, which travelled that route, for many years. She was a stewardess on the *Olympic* when, in 1911, it collided with the *H.M.S. Hawke* off the Isle of Wight. In 1912, she was transferred to the *Titanic*.

After the sinking, she sent a telegram from New York to her brother-in-law in Belfast. It contained only one word: 'SAFE'. Mary returned to the United Kingdom on the *Lapland* and spent some time with friends in the south of England before travelling back to Belfast via Liverpool.

In Belfast, Mary recounted her adventures on the *Titanic* to eager reporters. She had nothing but praise for Thomas Andrews and John Simpson. She said that Andrews had realised the gravity of the accident from the first, and by his face she had seen how serious events were; he had worked 'nobly and like a true hero', going around the vessel to see that all women had lifebelts before they went on deck to take their place in the lifeboats. She said that he had thought of everyone except himself. When she had last seen him, he was helping women and children to get into the boats, urging them not to hesitate, as there was not a moment to lose.

Mary said that she had seen John Simpson, the assistant surgeon, about ten minutes after the accident occurred, and had a short conversation with him. She had asked John if he thought it was serious, and he had replied that he was afraid it was. He had then left Mary to attend to any medical emergencies, and she never saw him again. Mary said that John was a splendid fellow and was extremely popular with all on board; he had done his work 'nobly and unselfishly', and had been most helpful to all passengers who required his aid.

Mary left the *Titanic* in Lifeboat No. 12, having given up her place in another boat to a woman passenger. Mary said there had been about sixty or seventy people in Boat No. 12; the people on the overturned lifeboat, including Charles Lightoller and Belfast men John Haggan and Thomas Dillon, had all transferred into her boat. Mary described the boat as being crowded to the point of danger and very un-comfortable. She added that it was very fortunate that the weather had been calm, as otherwise they might not have reached the *Carpathia*.

While returning to England on board the *Lapland*, Mary wrote to her sister Maggie Brown, who lived in Bangor. In the letter, Mary (who signs her name as 'May') describes the night of the sinking. She also tells of the kindness of a Mrs McWilliams of New York, who took her to Brooklyn and gave her money and clothes:

Did you ever hear of such kindness from strangers. Of course I took them on condition that I would pay them back again.[31]

Describing the night of the sinking, she wrote:

> You will be glad to know that dreadful night I never lost my head once. When she struck at a quarter to twelve and the engines stopped I knew very well something was wrong. Doctor Simpson [John Simpson, assistant surgeon, from Belfast] came and told me the mails were afloat. I knew things were pretty bad. He brought Miss Marsden [another stewardess] and I into his room and gave us a little whiskey and water. I laughed and asked him if he thought we needed it, and he said we should. He asked me if I was afraid, I replied I was not. He said well spoken like a true Ulster girl. He had to hurry away to see if there was anyone hurt. We helped him on with his great coat, I never saw him again.

Mary did not mention the incident with the whiskey when talking to the press! Later in the letter, she recalls meeting Thomas Andrews:

> Poor Mr Andrews came along, I read in his face all I wanted to know. He saw me knocking at some of the passengers doors, he said that was right, told me to see if they had life belts on and to get one for myself and go on deck. He was a brave man. Last time I saw and heard him was about an hour later, helping to get women and children into the boats.... So Mr Andrews met his fate like a true hero realizing his great danger, and gave up his life to save the women and the children of the *Titanic*.

She also described a previous encounter with Andrews and Doctor O'Loughlin.

> I was talking to him [Andrews] on the Friday night previous as he was going to dinner. The dear old doctor was waiting for him on the stair landing and calling him by his christian name Tommy, Mr Andrews seemed loath to go, as he wanted to talk about home, he was telling me his father was ill and Mrs A. was not so well. I congratulated him on the beauty and perfection of the ship. He said the part he did not like the *Titanic* was taking us further away from home every hour.... His face struck me at the time as having a very sad expression.

Of her escape, Mary wrote:

> I went on deck the second time, and one of our little bill boys recognized me, and pointing to a crowded boat said, Miss Sloan that's your boat No. 12. I said, child, how do you know, I will wait for another.... I saw Captain Smith getting excited, passengers would not have noticed, I did. There was a big crush behind me.... I was pushed into the boat, I believe it was one of the last ones to leave.... We were in the boats all night. I took a turn to row, the women said I encouraged them, I was pleased. We picked up 30 men.... I only hope I shall never have a like experience again.

She concluded by saying that she was paid a compliment by Second Officer Charles Lightoller, who said she would make a sailor. She signed the letter 'Your loving sister May.'

W. Swann
(LOST)

In 1912, Mr Swann was forty-six years old. He was employed by the White Star Line as a bedroom steward, and was paid £3.15s. per month.

He joined the *Titanic* on 4 April 1912, transferring from the *Olympic*, and he gave his last address as 174 Shirley Road, Southampton. His instructions were to be on board no later than 6.00 a.m. on 10 April (sailing day).

In the official lists, his name is recorded as 'W. Gwann', but a Belfast newspaper gives his name as Swann and states that he was from Belfast. This discrepancy could be explained by poor handwriting, although his entry in the Articles of Agreement is quite legible.

Richard Turley
(LOST)

Richard was born in 1877 and was employed by the White Star Line as a fireman. His pay in 1912 was £6 per month. Richard lived at 12 Lettuce Hill, Divis Street, Belfast, with his wife Eliza, and their daughter Annie.

After being discharged from the *Carrigan Head*, he signed on the *Titanic* on 29 March 1912, and travelled with the ship on her sea trials and on the trip to Southampton. He rejoined the ship on 6 April, boarding her at 6.00 a.m. with the other firemen. His wife was later awarded £237.12s. for the daughter and herself in an action against Ismay Immrie and Co. Ltd.

Ennis Hastings Watson
(LOST)

Ennis was employed by Harland and Wolff as an apprentice electrician, and travelled on the *Titanic* as a member of the guarantee group.

He was born in 1894, and in 1912 was only eighteen. He lived at 75 Madrid Street, Belfast. His father was described as an agent who had an office at Victoria Street, Belfast.

Ennis had been a student at the Belfast Municipal Technical Institute for five years, studying art, electrical wiring and fitting. He had earned awards in the examinations held by the Board of Education in 1908–1909 and in the City and Guilds examinations of 1909–1910; he seemed to have a brilliant future before him.

Patrick Morgan

All of the people listed in this chapter sailed on the *Titanic* on her voyage from Southampton towards New York and were on board her when she struck the iceberg. However, there is one Ulsterman whose connection with the ship

Page from the Belfast signing-on log. Patrick Morgan's name can be seen on line 43.

(Public Record Office of Northern Ireland Document No. TRANS 2A/45/381C)

is well worth recording even though he was not on board at the time of the disaster. Patrick Morgan was a member of the *Titanic*'s crew when she sailed from Belfast to Southampton. What makes his story unique is that the fact that he chose to return to Belfast rather than continuing on board the *Titanic* — and that he used the sinking of the ship to defend himself in court.

134

Patrick was a twenty-six-year-old fireman, married, and living at Shore Street, Belfast. In early March 1912, he returned to Belfast, having served on the *Carrigan Head*. On 29 March, he signed on to serve on the *Titanic* as a fireman. He reported for duty on 1 April, at 4.00 a.m., and took part in the *Titanic*'s sea trials in Belfast Lough and the Irish Sea on 2 April. That evening, he sailed for Southampton on board the *Titanic*.

For reasons known only to himself, however, Patrick flatly refused to go any further than Southampton on board the *Titanic*. He bade farewell to her and returned to Belfast.

On his arrival back in Belfast, he was issued with a summons to appear before the Belfast Custody Court on 26 April, on a charge of assaulting his wife. Before the case was heard, the *Titanic* sank — an event which Patrick was to use in his defence.

On 26 April, the resident magistrate, Sir Andrew Newton-Brady, presided over the court; Mr Spiller was the prosecuting counsel, and Mr John Osbourne represented Patrick. In his opening address, Mr Osbourne informed the magistrate that Patrick Morgan was the son of a distinguished old soldier, and that he had been extremely lucky. He had been due to sail on the *Titanic* (which, as we know, was not true), and if he had done so, he would probably have been dead before the date of the hearing.

Mrs Morgan was called to give evidence and said that she did not wish to press the case; she was simply relieved that Patrick had not gone down with the *Titanic*, and that she had him home safe and well. Following Mrs Morgan's evidence, the magistrate dismissed the case and told Patrick that he should be thankful for his escape from certain death. He was also told to make a resolution never to appear before the court again.

We can only wonder what Patrick's fate would have been if he had not used the *Titanic* disaster in his defence in court.

All the signatures included in this chapter are from the signing-on logs at Belfast and Southampton. Crown copyright material in the Public Record Office of Northern Ireland is reproduced by permission of Dr A.P.W. Malcomson, the Deputy Keeper of Records (PRO Belfast Document TRANS 2A/45/381 A–C). All discharge certificates included in this chapter are from the 'Titanic Log', by permission of The National Archives, ref. BT100/259.

CHAPTER 12

Titanic **Buildings**

Throughout Northern Ireland, there are buildings with links to the *Titanic*. Apart from obvious examples such as the office block, drawing offices and time offices at Harland and Wolff, there are buildings such as the Royal Belfast Academic Institute, where Thomas Andrews and John Simpson were educated; Queens University, where Simpson took his medical degree; and the Municipal Technical Institute, where Albert Ervine and Ennis Watson studied. Belfast City YMCA has a memorial plaque to Ervine, who attended their Bible class. The Lord Mayor of Belfast has a bathroom modelled on a stateroom of the *Titanic*. The Ulster Reform Club has a memorial plaque to Andrews. The Empire Bar, in Botanic Avenue in Belfast, has a cabinet devoted to displaying various *Titanic* and White Star Line memorabilia. There is even an Orange Lodge named in memory of Thomas Andrews.

Among all of these *Titanic*-related buildings, however, there are two which stand out from the others: Ormiston House, the Belfast home of Lord Pirrie, and the Thomas Andrews Junior Memorial Hall in Comber, County Down.

Ormiston House

Ormiston House, a large, beautiful house built in the Scottish Baronial style, occupies a delightful setting in the heart of East Belfast. Entry to the house and gardens is along a short driveway from Wandsworth Road. The house is surrounded by large, secluded grounds, its lawns laid out with bushes and trees. The view from the roof of the house takes in nearly all of Belfast, spreading out to Cave Hill in the north of the city. The gantries and cranes of the Harland and Wolff shipyard can be seen over the rows of trees in the gardens.

The last occupants of the building were the Police Authority for Northern Ireland, but the property, which is a listed building, is currently the subject of a planning application to convert it into luxury apartments.

The house was originally built in Glasgow, Scotland, in 1867. It was brought over to its present site by Coombe Reed, a wealthy Scotsman who was associated with shipbuilding in Belfast. It was occupied by Edward Harland, later to become Sir Edward, who used it as his Belfast home until his death on Christmas Eve 1895.

William Pirrie then bought the house, and used it as a Belfast base for himself and his wife Margaret. At that time the entrance to the house and

136

Above: Ormiston House. Below: Belfast from the roof of Ormiston House. (Both — author's collection)

Right: Lord and Lady Pirrie on the doorstep of Ormiston House. (Ulster Folk and Transport Museum.
Photograph reproduced courtesy the Trustees of National Museums Northern Ireland)

The main staircase at Ormiston House.
(Author's collection)

grounds was via a long private avenue which ran up through the lawns from Belmont Road. The gatehouse is still in use today, as a private home.

The gardener, Thomas Griffin, who occupied the front lodge, would not have found his skill fully tested, as Pirrie had the lawns laid out without a single flower or flowerbed. The whole extent of the grounds was given over to wide stretches of grass, and the driveway was bordered with rows of fir trees.

Entering the house is like stepping back in time. Here, at the porch in front of the main door, the photograph of Lord and Lady Pirrie was taken, with His Lordship resplendent in his uniform of Privy Councillor.

Quote on outside wall, Ormiston House.
(Author's collection)

The entrance hall and stairway are finished in fine oak panelling, and the ceilings are of intricate plasterwork. A dog-leg staircase rises from the entrance hall with its welcoming marble fireplace; the workmanship and finishing of the newel posts, spandrels and banister-rails are of the highest standard. At the head of the staircase is a beautiful three-panelled leaded bow-window; various mottoes are engraved upon it, in French, Latin and Irish, including 'Dieu et Mon Droit' and 'Nemo Me Impune Lacessit'.

Various proverbs and sayings are carved on stone tablets set in the walls of the house: 'Truth will prevail'; 'What shall be, shall'; 'Do right and trust in God'; 'He that thoules overcomes'. Lord Pirrie — who, throughout his life, carried a little book of maxims which had been given to him by his mother, Eliza — was, no doubt, fond of these sayings; perhaps he added them to his collection.

While some of the rooms have been divided, the character of the house is still there, in details such as the fine carving on some of the wooden surrounds of the fireplaces. One of the toilets still holds the original Shanks wash-hand basin and toilet, complete with wooden seat and lid.

Behind the house are outbuildings which were once used as stables, and a secluded door leading to what was probably a kitchen garden.

In 1897, the house was visited by royalty: the Duke and Duchess of York, who would later become King George V and Queen Mary, visited Ormiston on 8 September. Lord Pirrie, who was then in his second year of office as Lord Mayor of Belfast, invited 10,000 Sunday school children to meet with the Duke and Duchess. During their visit, the Duke and Duchess planted two cypress trees, which still stand behind the house a century later.

William James Pirrie died on 7 June 1924, on board the *SS Ebro*, off the South American coast. His body was embalmed, brought back to the United Kingdom on board his beloved *SS Olympic*, and taken to his favourite place — Belfast. On the morning of 23 June 1924, Pirrie's body was taken from Ormiston House to his final resting place in Belfast City Cemetery.

Following Lord Pirrie's death, the house was occupied for a short time by George Cumming of Harland and Wolff, and then it was placed for sale on the open market. Pirrie had stipulated in his will that the house, if possible, should be used for educational purposes, and in 1927 it was bought for use as a preparatory school for Campbell College. In 1975 it was purchased by the Police Authority for Northern Ireland, who occupied the building until 1996. The Northern Ireland Assembly, with a view to using it as office space, then purchased the building. This option was never followed up and the building as stated is being considered for a change of use to apartments, with houses being built in the grounds.

Andrews Hall from road bridge. Andrews Mill is on the right

(Author's collection)

The Thomas Andrews Junior Hall

Following the *Titanic* disaster and the death of Thomas Andrews, the residents of the town and district of Comber decided to erect a hall to his memory. Donations from the public were called for, and a steering committee was set up to oversee the project. It was decided that the hall would be built on the Ballygowan Road in Comber, near to both the Andrews family home at Ardara, and the linen mill owned by the family.

The architects responsible for designing the hall were Messrs Young and Mackenzie, and the builders were Messrs Courtney Bros. The first sod on the site was cut by Thomas's young daughter, Elizabeth Law Barbour Andrews — Elba, as the family called her — on 2 October 1913. On 13 January 1914, a memorial stone was laid by Thomas's mother Eliza.

The Thomas Andrews Junior Hall was officially opened on the afternoon of Friday, 29 February 1915, by Thomas Andrews' widow, Helen. Because of the First World War, the Andrews family had requested that the opening ceremony be informal and private. In opening the hall, Mrs Andrews thanked all those who had contributed to the cost of the building and said that she deeply appreciated the generosity which had been shown; she also thanked the trustees and committee who had overseen the whole project. She said that it was very gratifying to have been asked to open the hall, and she hoped that it would be of benefit to the people of Comber.

The hall, which is built of dressed stone, is probably one of the finest buildings in any provincial town in Ireland. In 1915, the ground floor held a billiard room, a reading room, a minor hall, a committee room, a kitchen and toilets. Two stone dog-leg staircases run from the entrance lobby, on the ground floor, to the first-floor main hall, which seats about seven hundred people. The main hall holds a stage, and at the front, under a large leaded window, is a gallery. The ceiling is of king-post design with exposed timbers.

On the first floor is a large plaque in memory of Thomas. The inscription details his life and ends with the words:

> When with tragic suddenness the call came he died, as he lived, faithful to his duties, and gave his life that others might be saved.

In 1915, the grounds surrounding the hall were laid out as a park.

Over the years, the hall has been used for many community events, including a weekly dance. Eventually the hall was taken over by the South-Eastern Education and Library Board and used as a primary school, under the name 'Andrews Memorial Primary School'. As the numbers of children increased, a new school was built adjoining the hall, which is still used by the school.

Every ten years, the school puts on an exhibition of the children's work telling the *Titanic* story, and this always draws a large crowd. In 1992, the items on display included the morning suit in which Thomas Andrews was married. In late 1993, another special event was held in the hall, when the Belfast *Titanic* Society played host to a group of American *Titanic* enthusiasts who were on a tour of the United Kingdom.

CHAPTER 13

'I Saw the *Titanic*'

Between 1907, when Bruce Ismay and William Pirrie first hatched the idea of the Olympic-class liners, and 1912, when the *Titanic* left Belfast as the largest movable man-made object ever, literally hundreds of thousands of people must have caught sight of the ship.

In 1912, fifteen thousand people were employed in the shipyard, and these people would have passed No. 3 slip, where the *Titanic* was being constructed, on a daily basis. The residents of the side-streets of Lower Newtownards Road would have witnessed every step of her majestic rise. Anyone crossing Queen's Bridge over the River Lagan had only to pause for a moment to see for themselves the pride of Harland and Wolff. The launch of the ship, on 31 May 1911, was watched by thousands, and the roar of their cheers as the ship was launched must have been audible for miles.

Sadly, however, none of those hundreds of thousands who saw the Titanic first-hand are still alive today. One major stumbling-block in any research is always the inevitable passage of time — the fact that it quickly becomes too late to ask questions. However, in the 1990s, when I first put this book together, there were still a few people in their nineties who remembered those days leading up to 2 April 1912. The clarity with which they recalled those long-ago days was astonishing, and they were happy to share their memories.

Mollie Cornforth

Mollie was born in January 1906. Her father, Samuel A. Armstrong, was a charge hand engineer at Harland and Wolff. Before the *Titanic* left Belfast, he took young Mollie to see the ship. 'I remember standing on cobblestones, looking up at the side of this big ship,' she says. 'I could see a lot of people on the deck, and there was so much noise from the crowds.' Mollie married Cyril Drysdale, who worked in the drawing office at the shipyard; she was later married again, to a Yorkshireman, Leslie Cornforth.[1]

Harry Currie

Harry was born on 31 January 1897. At the time of the *Titanic*'s construction, Harry was working at the 'wee yard' of Workman and Clark. His father was an upholsterer who was working on the furniture of the *Titanic*; Harry was asked to join him, but declined and stayed with Workman and Clark. Each day, as he travelled to work, he saw the *Titanic* increasing in size.[2]

Bob Currie (pictured right — Belfast Titanic Society)

Bob was born in 1900. In May 1911, his father took him to see the launch of the *Titanic*. Bob remembered it well: 'I can remember my father taking me down Queen's Road to see the big ship *Titanic* being launched. There were so many people that I couldn't really see, but I remember the roar of the crowd when the ship was launched.' Bob's father also pointed out the *Olympic*, which was handed over to the White Star Line on the same day.

Bob also saw the *Titanic* leave Belfast on 2 April, but he recalled: 'My only regret is that at the time I didn't have a better view of the ship leaving — say a view from Cavehill, Holywood, Carrickfergus or Orlock.'[3]

Bob passed away in 1997.

Tommy McBride (pictured right — Belfast Titanic Society)

Tommy was born in 1905 in East Belfast, in the shadow of the Harland and Wolff shipyard. His brothers and uncles were all employed in the shipyard in various capacities. As a young child, Tommy had only to look across the mud flats at the bottom of Newtownards Road to see the Arroll Gantry and the *Titanic*. Many a time, he crossed those flats to gaze at the new ship's progress. He remembered watching the new ship leave Belfast on 2 April 1912.[4]

When Tommy was fifteen, he too joined the workforce of Harland and Wolff. Sadly, he died in 1998.

William McQuitty

William was born in Bangor, County Down, in 1905. As a boy of five, he was taken to witness the launch of the *Titanic* on 31 May 1911. He recalls: 'Every ship in the Lough sounded its siren, the noise drowning the roar of the piles of restraining anchors as they dragged along the ground. Slowly gathering speed, the *Titanic* moved smoothly down the slip, and a minute later was plunging into the water and raising a huge wave. I felt a great lump in my throat and an enormous pride in being an Ulsterman.'[5]

William went on to become the founder managing director of Ulster Television. He is best known as the producer of the classic *Titanic* film, *A Night to Remember*.

144

Francis John Parkinson

(pictured left — Belfast Titanic Society)

John was born in January 1907. His father, who was also called John, worked as a joiner in Harland and Wolff and had been involved in the construction of the *Titanic*. One day, when young John was four years old, his father took him out of Sunday school and they took the tram to Queen's Road from their Grosvenor Road home to see the *Titanic* in the slip before the launch. According to John:

> I could hardly believe that I was going to see the great *Titanic*. As we got off the tram, many other workers were taking the opportunity to show their families this great showpiece. I can well remember that first sight of the great mammoth hull of steel perched in the great gantry — a fantastic sight. My father explained that the ship would be launched into the water shortly. 'But Dad,' I asked him, 'how will that big boat stay up in the water?' I have always remembered his answer. 'Johnny,' he said, 'that big ship will always stay up in the water.' How wrong he was.'

In January 1912, as a birthday treat, John's father took him to see the ship a second time, as she was undergoing her final fitting-out at the outfitting wharf at Queen's Road. By that stage, the ship would have been almost complete. John remembers it well.

> I couldn't believe my eyes. There was this huge ship with its four funnels and its gleaming white decks, with great activity going on all around her. Painters were busy varnishing the bridge and painting the ship's side. Everyone was busy making it ready for its trip to America.

Less than ten weeks later, in the early evening of 2 April, John's father brought him to a vantage point on Belfast Lough, near Greencastle, to witness the *Titanic*'s final departure from Belfast.

> We saw the great boat being towed out by twelve tugs. They pulled her up Belfast Lough to near Holywood. Then we saw black smoke belching from her funnels, and we could hear the great roar from her engines and the noise of her propellers turning. At last the ship was on her way under her own steam, and as we watched her head away we waved our handkerchiefs and sang 'Land of Hope and Glory'. It was really good-bye to her forever.

John followed in his father's footsteps and went to work for Harland and Wolff as a joiner. Later in life he taught woodwork in a secondary school; one pupil recalled that Mr Parkinson always had time for his students, and treated them just like young apprentices. Given John's interest in the *Titanic*, it is no surprise that he was for over 10 years the President of the Ulster and then renamed Belfast Titanic Society. John passed away in 2006.[6]

Gordon Roberts

(pictured right — author's collection)

Gordon was born in 1906. In 1908, his father, who was a coastguard, was posted at the Coastguard Station at Carrickfergus, which overlooked Belfast Lough. Gordon remembers his father taking him to the watchroom in the Station on 2 April 1912.

> My father took me to the Station to see the *Titanic* going past. He told me that she was a big new ship and she was going out on her sea trials. I also saw her coming back into Belfast after her trials in the late evening. I was ship-mad at that age, and I remember my father telling me that the *Titanic* was as long as a football field. I also saw her leave Belfast for Southampton.

Gordon's elder brothers worked as lifeboat builders in the Harland and Wolff shipyard. He also worked in the shipyard for a brief period, but eventually went to work for Belfast City Corporation on the buses until his retirement.[7]

Paddy Scott

(pictured right— author's collection)

Paddy was born in 1907 and lived with his parents and six brothers at the Coastguard Station at Cloghy, County Down. His father was an ex-navy man who was then employed as the Chief Officer at the Station, so Paddy had a grandstand view of the *Titanic* as she sailed past on 2 April 1912.

> There was nothing as exciting as the thought of seeing the greatest liner in the world, which everyone had been talking about for weeks. My eldest brother had been an engineering apprentice and had told us all about 'the big boat, 401'. We first saw her coming from the Portavogie direction and moving slowly. We all cheered. I recall being fascinated by the big black chimneys, as I called them. I have never seen as many people as were gathered to watch the ship sail past; they came from farms and villages inland, including some from Ballgalget, where I went to infant school. I remember my father giving me sixpence, as money was passed to children to celebrate the great event. My father told me that it was 'a day to remember', and remember it I did — the great ship mirrored on the horizon....

Paddy later joined Ulster Television and became a producer; in 1962, he made a television documentary on the *Titanic*.[8]

Hans Williamson

(pictured left — Williamson family)

Hans was born in 1900. Before the *Titanic* left Belfast, his parents took him to see the ship. He recalls:

> Standing on the jetty, I thought that I could nearly reach out and touch the great big ship, it was so large.

Hans Williamson worked in both of Belfast's shipyards, Workman and Clark, and Harland and Wolff, and was later employed in the Purchasing Office of Harland and Wolff.[9]

Photograph reproduced courtesy the Trustees of National Museums Northern Ireland.

CHAPTER 14

The Reality of the *Titanic*

The scene is easy to imagine. It was an evening in 1907, and William Pirrie, the chairman of Harland and Wolff, was entertaining his friend Joseph Bruce Ismay, the chairman of the White Star Line, at dinner in his London home. The dinner was over, and the two men — the epitome of all that was expected of gentlemen of the Edwardian era — would probably have sat down with glasses of port. The talk would soon have come around to the competition that the White Star Line was facing from the other major British shipping company, the Cunard Line. In 1899, when White Star had put the *Oceanic* into service, they had been in the vanguard of technology. The *Oceanic* had been the marvel of her time; passengers had loved her, and she had made Ismay and his company world-famous. But in 1906, Cunard had launched the magnificent *Lusitania*, and her sister ship, the *Mauretania*, would soon be completed. Since the *Lusitania* had been introduced, the number of passengers travelling with the White Star Line had fallen.

Ismay had to find a way to regain the lead against Cunard in the intense competition over the North Atlantic crossing.

The two men lingering over their port did not realise that the decision they were about to make would have ramifications beyond their wildest dreams; after that night, their lives would never be the same again.

Their decision was to build a new breed of liner — ships which would be the largest floating objects ever to be launched into Belfast's River Lagan. The ships of their vision would boast luxurious passenger accommodation: a Parisian café, a swimming pool, a gymnasium, electric lifts, staterooms that would be the envy of many a manor house, and not one but two grand staircases upon which the wealthy could make their entrances as they descended for dinner. These new leviathans, which Pirrie and Ismay were discussing and sketching, were to be called the Olympic-class liners, and their names would reflect their greatness — they would be called the *Olympic*, the *Titanic* and the *Britannic*. After that night, the world of shipping would never be the same again.

Within days, Pirrie returned to his Belfast shipyard. He would have called a meeting of his various heads of department, announced the result of his discussions with Ismay and given the brief to the waiting managers. He would have specified the size of each vessel, the number of engines, the type of boilers — every detail which he and the White Star Line wanted the new ships to have.

CHAPTER 14

The Reality of the *Titanic*

The finest materials were to be used, and every effort was to be made to ensure the passengers' comfort. Mahogany and teak, two inches thick and inlaid with mother-of-pearl, would adorn the rooms of the wealthy; wall panels in the first-class bedrooms would be hand-painted by craftsmen at the shipyard; a local firm would supply palm trees to stand in the Verandah Lounge. These new liners would be the largest the world had ever seen — Harland and Wolff were determined that they should also be the finest.

For Belfast, the contract to build these new ships would have been a godsend. Over the next five or six years, more than fifteen thousand men and women would be employed by Harland and Wolff.

On 20 October 1910, the *Olympic*, the first of the three sisters, was launched. She was handed over to her owners, the White Star Line, on the same day that her younger sister the *Titanic* was launched — 31 May 1911. The *Olympic* entered service to great acclaim; and the *Titanic* was finally completed and handed over to her owners on 2 April 1912. Her maiden voyage was scheduled to begin on 10 April.

In their publicity for the Olympic-class liners, the White Star Line said that, because of their design and their watertight bulkheads, they were practically unsinkable. The press, who disliked any qualifying statements, stated that the ships were unsinkable. However, in the midst of all the excitement and praise surrounding the new ships, there were some who felt concern.

According to Board of Trade regulations, the number of lifeboats a ship was required to carry was determined by the tonnage of the vessel, not by the number of passengers she was registered to carry. The *Titanic* was certified to carry 3,547 passengers and crew members; her sixteen lifeboats provided space for 979 people. The four collapsible boats brought the total amount of available lifeboat places to 1,167 — 32 per cent of the ship's registered passenger capacity — which meant that the amount of lifeboat space on board the *Titanic* actually exceeded Board of Trade requirements. Why should the White Star Line use up valuable deck space on extra lifeboats, when the odds against anything going wrong were a million to one?

When Bruce Ismay boarded the *Titanic* in Southampton in April 1912, disaster was the last thing on his mind. But at 11.40 p.m. on the night of 14 April, the worst happened: the *Titanic* grazed an iceberg for over 300 feet of her length. Within seconds, she was mortally wounded. Ismay must have cursed the decision that had been made about the lifeboats. Just over seven hundred people were to survive the maiden voyage of his and Pirrie's dream.

Ismay himself survived the sinking, but neither he nor the White Star Line ever really recovered. Ismay died, practically a recluse, in 1937. Pirrie — whose hair apparently turned white after the disaster — had died some years earlier, in 1924.

What lessons, then, have been learned from the *Titanic*? The British Government held an inquiry into the disaster, headed by the Wreck Commissioner, Lord Mersey. In his report, of 30 July 1912, Mersey and his assessors made twenty-four recommendations to the government with regard to issues of safety at sea. Shortly afterwards, the Safety of Life at Sea convention implemented many of these recommendations, including one which required ships to provide lifeboat space for all of those on board. This convention eventually led to the International Maritime Organisation, which now rules on safety at sea and strives to make sea travel safer for all.

In 1912, thousands turned out to watch the *Titanic* leave Belfast after her sea trials. The ship had been just over thirty-seven months in the making. The workforce of Harland and Wolff had put their best efforts and their best materials into the vessel that was to show the world that if you wanted a good ship built, you should come to Belfast. As she sailed down Belfast Lough for the last time, in the early evening of 2 April, adults and children burst into song and pulled out handkerchiefs to wave goodbye to their creation, the *Titanic*.

When news of the disaster came through, these same people, who had witnessed history only a few days earlier, were openly reduced to tears. Their finest work lay at the bottom of the Atlantic.

The sinking of the *Titanic* is not among the top ten shipping disasters of all time. It was the worst maritime disaster of 1912; but since then, as ships have increased in size and tonnage, there have been worse disasters at sea. In January 1945, the *Wilhelm Gustloff* was lost with over 7,700 people on board. More recently, in December 1987, the *Dona Paz* collided with the motor vessel *Victor* near the Philippines, and over 3,000 people lost their lives. Yet the *Titanic* still springs to mind when shipping disasters are mentioned.

The year 1912 was part of the pre-First World War 'Golden Age'; technology was progressing in leaps and bounds, making new conquests on land, in the air and at sea. In April 1912, the *Titanic* was the new wonder of the world, and the pride of the Harland and Wolff shipyard and of Belfast, her birthplace.

Una Reilly, co-founder and current Chair of the Belfast Titanic Society, summed it up perfectly when she said: 'What happened was a disaster. The *Titanic* was not.'

Did You Know...?

Titanic Trivia — Facts about the *Titanic*'s Belfast Connection

- It was Harland and Wolff's policy to make small payments to the captain and chief engineer of each new ship handed over, to enable the recipients to purchase small souvenirs of their visit to Belfast.

- A masseur, Herr Egger, was employed by Harland and Wolff for a period of three months, for a fee of £24.17s.6d. A Mr A. Cameron, the repair manager, had sprained his ankle; after six visits to Herr Egger, he was fit to return to his duties.

- James Harkness and Company were engaged to transport heavy or bulky items to the shipyard from their local manufacturers or from the port. The cost to the shipyard was 13d. per ton, less a discount of 2% for prompt payment.

- Before the *Titanic* sailed, John Kelly and Company, Coal Merchants, made several deliveries of coal for her departure. The final delivery was made on 25 March 1912, when two hundred tons of Scottish steam coal, costing 35s. a ton, were placed in No. 2 stokehold.

- A new electrical sub-station had to be constructed at the fitting-out wharf to meet the demand for electricity during the fitting out of the *Olympic* and the *Titanic*.

- The shipyard purchased two cars, which were parked at the main gate, for the purpose of transporting any injured workmen to hospital. Outside working hours, these cars were available for hire.

- In 1911, the *SS Mauretania* suffered slight collision damage in the Mersey. The possibility of bringing her to Belfast for repair in the Thompson graving dock was considered, but this was not possible, as the Victoria Channel was not deep enough to accommodate her.

- In 1907, management at the shipyard witnessed a display of a new technique — steel-plate welding — by the Thermite Company.

- Once a ship had been contracted for, the shipyard initiated a process called the 'order to proceed': Pirrie wrote to both the shipyard and the engine works, giving them details of the new vessel — including its length, breadth, and depth and brief details of its engines — and stating at which slip the vessel was to be built.

- Owners paid the shipyard for their vessels in instalments. There were usually four instalments: the first was paid when the ship's double bottom was framed and the boiler plates were in place; the second, when the vessel was plated and one-third riveted, cylinders and bedplates had been cast, boiler shells had been riveted and furnaces had been delivered to the works; the third, when the vessel had been launched, the deck had been laid, cabin work was in progress, and masts, spars and machinery were ready to go on board; and the fourth and final payment was made when the ship had been completed and delivered to the owners in good working order.

- The workforce at the shipyard was varied. In 1912, some of the main trades were:

Platers	Riveters	Caulkers
Angle-smiths	Holders-On	Shipwrights
Joiners	Blacksmiths	Tinsmiths
Drillers	Hole cutters	Sheet Ironworkers
Painters	Sailmakers	Stagers
Electrical Wiremen	Boatbuilders	Labourers
Brass Moulders	Plumbers	Fitters
Cranemen	Decorators	Woodturners

A basin trial was undertaken on the *Titanic* while she was still docked, before 2 April 1912.

- Boilermakers and foundry labourers held a strike during the fitting out of the *Titanic*.

- In May 1911, Thomas Andrews was sent on the sea trials of the *Traffic* and the *Nomadic* — the tenders that would service the *Olympic* and the *Titanic* at Cherbourg. Today, the *Nomadic* being restored by the Nomadic Charitable Trust in Belfast, and is the only White Star Line vessel still afloat.

- In October 1912, Harland and Wolff discussed the idea of making the *Olympic* and the *Britannic* oil-burning, as an alternative to using coal.

- The position of foreman was a revered one in the shipyard. The following men were foremen in the shipyard in 1909, when the keel of the *Titanic* was laid, and also in April 1912, when she left Belfast:

Plater	John Williamson	Riveter	Thomas Kingan
Caulker	Hugh Hewitt	Smith	George Wood
Fitter	David Duncan	Shipwright	R.J. Keith
Joiner	John McClune	Painter	Henry Killop
Plumber	Robert Dyer	Electrician	T.H. Steadman
Decorator	J. Rose		

- The boilers of the *Titanic* were inspected in March 1909, her tonnage was measured in January 1910, and her freeboard was measured in November 1910.

- Local Belfast firms supplied the shipyard with materials used in the *Titanic*. Some of those firms were still in business in 2011; they are:

Irvin and Sellars	who supplied timber
J. Riddell and Company	who supplied buckets
Robert Kirk Limited	who supplied firebricks
James P. Corry	who supplied timber

- On that fateful night of 14–15 April 1912, many ships were in the North Atlantic and heard the distress call from the *Titanic*. One of these was the *Virginian*, whose radio operator, John McKenna Jr, was a native of Belfast.

- There were forty-four sacks of mail on board the *Titanic* when she sailed from Belfast.

- Messrs Whiting and Tedford, of Victoria Street, were the Belfast agents for the White Star Line. They received the first telegram to reach Ulster with the terrible news.

- A large bookcase which was to be located in the *Titanic*'s Library 2, on B Deck, arrived too late to be placed on board. It was bought by the mother of a Mrs Massey of Belfast; in 1955, it was purchased at auction by a Mr T. Hewitt of Belfast. Later, it was again put up for auction; it was purchased by H.M. Government, and now resides splendidly in a government building.

152

- The telephone number of Lord Pirrie's Belfast home, Ormiston, was 'KNOCK 68'.

- When a ship was under construction and still on the slipway prior to launch, Harland and Wolff referred to her by her number; only when the vessel was launched would the shipyard use her name. In other words, before her launch the *Titanic* was only referred to as '*SS 401*', while afterwards she was called '*SS Titanic*'.

- Belfast is well known for its numerous public houses. In 1912, there were bars in East Belfast called 'The Carpathia', 'The Brit' or 'Brittanic', and the 'White Star'.

- William Pirrie was quite a forward-looking individual. In late 1902, he decided that the growing mountains of paperwork and books in the shipyard should be reduced, and introduced a system of document disposal. In a memorandum dated January 1903, he ordered the destruction of old books and papers held by the various departments in the shipyard. Today, this elimination of old paperwork is widely practised by larger companies. Sadly, this — and the events of 15 April 1941, the anniversary of the sinking of the *Titanic*, when the shipyard was caught up in the Belfast blitz — have destroyed large parts of the *Titanic* era forever.

TELEGRAMS:
"Harland, Belfast."

ALL COMMUNICATIONS TO BE ADDRESSED TO THE FIRM.

Shipbuilding & Engineering Works,

Belfast, 8 January 1903.

Memorandum as to destruction of Old Books, Papers, etc.

To be destroyed.

X All Correspondence, i.e. Letters & Letter Books over 7 years old.

X Excepting Private Letter Books & Letters)
)
   constituting Contracts, kept in safe.)

All subsidiary Books, such as Returns from Time)
) over 5 years old.
Offices, Stores and Gates.)

Wages Books, Invoices & First Cost Abstracts   over 10 years old.

Not to be destroyed at any time.

Ledgers, Journals, Invoice Books outwards, and press copy Books of Accounts, Builder's certificates, etc., also Cash Books, Bill Books and Staff Wages Books. Receipts and Vouchers.

W.J. Pirrie

The above instructions to remain in force until countermanded and to be acted upon periodically once a year.

Letter from W.J. Pirrie of Harland and Wolff.

(Public Record Office of Northern Ireland, D2805/Misc/3)

SS *Titanic* Chronology

Compiled by Victoria and Stephen Cameron

1636	A 150-ton ship is built by Presbyterian clergymen in Belfast.
1791	In July; William Ritchie, a Scot, founds the first shipyard in Belfast. His first vessel is the 300-ton *Hibemia*.
1820	Two shipyards are operating on the banks of the Lagan; Ritchie's and another one owned by Ritchie's brother Hugh and Ills partner Alexander McLaine. This second yard is the first in Ireland to launch a steamboat — the *Belfast*.
1824	Ritchie's yard is purchased by Charles Connell and renamed Charles Connell and Sons.
1838	In December, a third shipyard, Kirwan and McCune, opens. It is situated further down the Lagan than the other two yards. Its vessels are launched into the Lagan. Kirwan and McCune launch the 114-ton schooner William and Mary.
1840	The Belfast Ballast Board starts to straighten the Lagan. The spoil is deposited at the east side of the river to form a 17-acre island which becomes known as Dargan's Island, after William Dargan, the main contractor. Captain William Pirrie is a member of the Ballast Board; his grandson, also called William, will later become the chairman of Harland and Wolff.
1847	Legislation reforms the Ballast Board into the Belfast Harbour Commissioners.
1849	Dargan's Island is renamed Queen's Island in honour of Queen Victoria.
1851	Kirwan and McCune (now Thompson and McCune) move their yard to Queen's Island.
1853	In September, the Belfast Harbour Commissioners agree to an iron shipyard being established at Queen's Island for Robert Hickson.
1854	In December, twenty-three-year-old Edward James Harland, who previously worked at shipyards on the Clyde, approaches Hickson for a Job. He is given the position of General Manager.
1858	In September, Edward Harland buys the yard from Hickson for £5,000, with the help of his uncle, Gustav Schwabe of Liverpool.
1859	In July, the first ship built by Harland is launched; it is a cargo ship, the *Venetian*, built for J. Bibby, Sons and Company.
1861	In April, Edward Harland takes on Schwabe's nephew, Gustav Wilheirn Wolff, as a partner.
1862	In January, Wolff's name is added to the shipbuilding yard, and the firm of Harland and Wolff is born. A hundred and fifty workers are employed, and a fifteen-year-old apprentice by the name of William Pirrie joins the yard.
1867	The White Star Line shipping company collapses, owing £527,000 to the bank. The company flag and goodwill are bought by Thomas Ismay for £1,000. Gustav Schwabe introduces Ismay to Wolff. Queen's Island is connected to East Belfast.
1869	In September, Ismay forms the Oceanic Steam Navigation Company, also known as the White Star Line.
1870	In August, Harland and Wolff's Ship No. 73, the *Oceanic*, is launched. It will be handed over to the Oceanic Steam Navigation Company in February 1871.
1874	William Pirrie and brothers Walter and Alexander Wilson are offered a partnership deal by Harland and Wolff.
1880	Harland andWolff set up their own engine works at Queen's Island. The young Joseph Bruce Ismay starts work for his father at the White Star Line.
1885	The first triple-expansion engine is designed by the Harland and Woltf engine works.
1889	A young 'gentleman apprentice' by the name of Thomas Andrews joins Harland and Wolff.
1891	Thomas Ismay takes on his son, Joseph Bruce, as a partner in the White Star Line.
1892	Thomas Ismay resigns from the White Star Line.
1893	William Pirrie is elected to the Belfast City Council and Belfast Harbour Commissioners Board.
1894	William Pirrie becomes managing director of the Harland and Wolff shipyard.
1895	Edward Harland dies. Pirrie becomes chairman of Harland and Wolff.
1896/1897	William Pirrie is made Lord Mayor of Belfast. He is admitted as a privy councillor for Ireland on 6 August 1897.
1898	On 14 January, the new *Oceanic*, the thirty-fifth ship built by Harland and Wolff for the White Star Line, is launched. On 21 July, William Pirrie is honoured as the first Freeman of Belfast. Morgan Robertson, a little-known American author, writes a novel called *Futility*. The story concerns a ship called the *Titan* which, on a voyage across the Atlantic, strikes an iceberg and sinks. The similarity between this story and future events was amazingly close in detail.
1902	The International Mercantile Marine Company, run by J. Pierpoint Morgan, successfully takes over the Oceanic Steam Navigation Company for £10 million. One of the directors of the new board is William Pirrie. The Belfast Harbour Commissioners agree to Pirre's request to begin construction of a new dry dock over 800 feet long. This dock will later be known as the Thompson Dry Dock. At the time, there appears to be no point in constructing a dock so large, as there are no existing ships that can use the full dock.
1904	Joseph Bruce Ismay becomes President of the International Mercantile Marine Company
1906	Gustav Wolff retires from Harland and Wolff. William Pirrie becomes controlling chairman of the yard. In July, Pirrie is made a baron.
1907	At a dinner party at William Pirrie's home in London, he and Bruce Ismay conceive the idea of building three large vessels with which to compete with the Cunard Line. These vessels, the Olympic-class liners, will be named the *Olympic*, the *Titanic* and the *Britannic*.
1908	In July, a contract letter, agreeing to the construction of the three Olympic-class liners, is signed. Harland

154

and Wolff are to build new slipways and purchase a new gantry for the construction of the ships.

On 16 December, the keel of Ship No. 400 — the SS *Olympic* — is laid at slip No.1 at Queen's Island.

1909   On 22 March, the keel of the second of the three sister ships — Ship No. 401, the SS *Titanic* — is laid at slip No.2 at Queen's Island.

1910   In March, Harland and Wolff and the White Star Line discuss the number of lifeboats to be fitted on the Olympic-class liners. Alexander Carlisle, a naval architect and director of the yard, initially suggests sixty-four boats, then thirty-two; finally it is agreed that each ship will have sixteen lifeboats and four collapsible boats.

On 20 October, Ship No.400, the *Olympic*, is launched. Her hull is specially painted white to highlight her immense size.

1911   On 31 May, ten thousand people gather — at vantage points including the top of the Albert Clock — to witness the launch of Ship No. 401, the *Titanic*, at thirteen minutes past noon.

The *Olympic* is handed over to the White Star Line. In July, Harland and Wolff and the White Star Line set the date on which the *Titanic* will begin her maiden voyage: 20 March 1912.

1911   On 20 September, the *Olympic*, captained by Edward J, Smith, collides with the *HMS Hawke* in Southampton and is brought back to Belfast for repairs. This accident delays the *Titanic's* maiden voyage.

1911   In October, the White Star Line officially announces the date of the *Titanic's* maiden voyage — 10 April 1912 — in the *London Times*.

1912   In January, the sixteen lifeboats built at
January   Harland and Wolff are installed under the Wellin davits on board the *Titanic*. This number meets the contemporary Board of Trade requirements; the fact that four collapsible boats are also installed means that the amount of lifeboat space on the Titanic exceeds the requirements by 10 per cent.

In the same month, the call sign for the new Marconi radio is issued to the ship as MUC. This will later be changed to MGY.

February In February, the *Titanic* is successfully dry-docked in the Thompson dry dock.

In the same month, the *Olympic* returns to Belfast to have her port propeller repaired,and the two sister ships are together for the last time.

26 March The crew for the *Titanic* begins arriving in Belfast. For a period of seven days, the *Titanic* has two captains, H.J. Haddock and EJ. Smith.

31 March The outfitting of the *Titanic* is complete. She is nearly identical to the *Olympic*, except in a few details, including extra staterooms and suites. The most notable difference is the glazing which encloses part of the *Titanic's* promenade deck.

1 April   The *Titanic's* sea trials are postponed because of bad weather.

2 April   6.00 am: the *Titanic's* sea trials begin. A fire breaks out in the coal hold in boiler room 6 of the ship. 8.00 pm: the trials are completed, and the *Titanic* sets sail for Southampton. Thomas Andrews leads the nine-man guarantee group from Harland and Wolff, which will travel to New York with the ship.

4 April   Just after midnight, the *Titanic* is successfully berthed at Southampton.

10 April 12 noon: Tugs pull RMS *Titanic* away from her berth. As she moves away, the suction from her propellers causes the *New York* to break her moorings, and a collision is barely averted.

Ill health stops William Pirrie travelling on the maiden voyage.

5.30 pm: The *Titanic* arrives at Cherbourg, France. Two tenders ferry 274 passengers, — including John Jacob Astor, the *Titanic's* richest passenger, and his eighteen-year-old bride Madeleine to the ship. Twenty-two passengers disembark.

11 April The *Titanic* arrives at Queenstown (later to be called Cobh), Ireland, her last port of call. A total of 120 passengers and their luggage are ferried out to the ship by tender.

Francis Browne (later to be ordained in the Jesuit order and become Father Browne) disembarks from the ship, taking with him his camera and photographs of life on board.

1.30 pm: The *Titanic* raises her starboard anchor and sets sail for New York, with about 2,206 passengers and crew members on board.

12 April The *Titanic* travels approximately 326 miles. The Marconi radio breaks down; the two operators, Bride and Philips, work to repair it.

13 April The ship travels 519 miles. Various vessels ahead of the *Titanic* report, by radio, sightings of ice. The *Rappahannock* reports heavy ice warnings.

The boiler room fire which started in Belfast is finally extinguished.

14 April The *Titanic* picks up many ice warnings transmitted by other ships, including one warning, from the *Mesaba*, which is never taken to the bridge.

11.40 pm: The two lookouts in the crow's nest, Fleet and Lee, see an iceberg in the path of the ship. They ring the ship's bell and inform the bridge. Officer Murdoch orders the helm hard a-starboard and the engines reversed, but the starboard side of the *Titanic* scrapes along the iceberg for over 300 feet. Five compartments are opened to the sea. Surprisingly, the total size of the opening is no greater than 12 square feet. The *Titanic* is doomed.

12.00 midnight: Thomas Andrews is asked to inspect the ship and report to Captain Smith. Andrews reports that the ship can stay afloat for less than two hours.

The radio room sends out a call for assistance. The *Titanic* is the first ship to use both the old distress call, 'CQD', and the new 'SOS'.

15 April At about 12.25 am, the *Carpathia*, nearly 60 miles away, becomes the nearest ship to answer the call.

12.25 am: Captain Smith gives the order to load the lifeboats with women and children.

The first boat, No. 7, is lowered some twenty minutes later, with only twenty-eight people in it.

Over the next two hours, the lifeboats are loaded; one boat — No.l, with Lord and Lady Duff Gordon on board — leaves the ship with only twelve people in it. Mr and Mrs Straus — a couple in their seventies, owners of Macy's, the world's largest department store — approach Boat No. 8; Mrs Straus is offered a place in the boat, but her husband is refused. Mrs Straus gets out of the boat, saying that she and her husband have spent all their lives together and now they will die together; and they walk back into the *Titanic*.

The body of Mr Straus is later recovered, but his wife's body is never seen again. 2.20 am: The *Titanic* starts to sink. The steerage passengers have been kept on the ship, and there are no lifeboats left for them. Slowly the bow of the Titanic disappears under the water and her stern lifts high into the night sky. The ship sinks, and around 1,500 lives are lost.

4.00 am: The *Carpathia* picks up the first survivors from the lifeboats. By around 8.30 am, all of the 705 survivors have been picked up. The last survivor to board the *Carpathia* is Second Officer Charles Lightoller.

18 April	The *Carpathia* arrives in New York and the *Titanic* survivors disembark.
	The White Star Line engages ships to search for, and recover, any bodies. Eventually 330 bodies will be recovered; the last one is that of James McGrady from Ulster.
April-May	An inquiry headed by Senator Smith is held in America.
May-June	The British Government holds an Inquiry headed by Lord Mersey. Various witnesses are called. Mersey's report makes twenty recommendations concerning safety of life at sea. A major convention will later be held, which will ultimately lead to the formation of the International Maritime Organisation.
October	The book, *Thomas Andrews, Shipbuilder,* by Shan Bullock, is published. This year also sees the publication of *The Deathless Story of the Titanic,* by Philip Gibbs, and an account of the disaster written by survivor Lawrence Beesley, who travelled second class.
1913	The first in-depth research on the *Titanic* disaster is published in a book entitled *The Truth about the Titanic,* by Colonel Archibald Gracie, who was a first-class passenger.
	In March, J. Pierpoint Morgan dies.
	In April, the third of the Olympic-class liners, the *Britannic,* is launched in Belfast.
	In June, Bruce Ismay stands down as chairman of the White Star Line.
1914	The First World War breaks out. The *Olympic* is called into service as a troop carrier.
	The *Britannic* is commandeered into service as a hospital ship; she is sunk in the Aegean Sea, having either hit a mine or been torpedoed. She never carried a fare-paying passenger for the White Star Line.
1920	In June, the Belfast *Titanic* Memorial is unveiled at Donegall Square North and dedicated by the Lord Lieutenant of Ireland.
1921	In July, William Pirrie is made Viscount Pirrie of Belfast.
1924	On 7 June, William Pirrie dies at sea, on board the *SS Ebro.* Following his death, Lord Kylsant, Chairman of the Royal Mail Steamship Company, took control of Harland and Wolff and of the White Star Line. He formed a new company, White Star Line Limited.
1924	On 23 June, the funeral of Viscount Pirrie left his

	Belfast home, Ormiston, pausing at Harland and Wolff. Pirrie was laid to rest at the Belfast Cemetery.
1929	The film *Atlantic,* a joint venture between England and Germany, is released.
1931	Captain Arthur Rostron of the *Carpathia* publishes his autobiography, *Home from the Sea.* It includes an account of his part in the rescue of the *Titanic* survivors.
1934	Cunard takes control of the White Star Line. The new company is called Cunard White Star Limited.
1935	*RMS Olympic,* which has been in service since 1911, is finally broken up for scrap.
	Second Officer Charles Herbert Lightoller recalls his involvement in the loss of the *Titanic* in his autobiography, *Titanic and Other Ships.*
1937	In October, J. Bruce Ismay, practically a recluse, dies following a stroke.
1943	The German Government backs a propaganda film entitled *Titanic.*
1948	The book, *Viscount Pirrie of Belfast,* is published by Herbert Jefferson.
1956	After twenty years of research, Walter Lord publishes the story of the *Titanic* in the book *A Night to Remember.* The book proves to be a bestseller.
1958	Walter Lord's book is turned into the classic film of the same name, produced by William McQuitty from Bangor, County Down.
1959	In November, the Belfast *Titanic* Memorial is moved to its present location at Donegall Square East.
1964	The American film, *The Unsinkable Molly Brown,* is released.
1979	Sir Lew Grade releases the film *Raise the Titanic,* which is based on Clive Cussler's book. Grade is later quoted as saying, 'It would have been cheaper to lower the Atlantic than to make this film.' Another American film, *SOS Titanic,* is also released.
1980	The first attempts are made to locate the wreck of the *Titanic.* An American entrepreneur, Jack Grimm, dreams of discovering the ship but fails to locate her.
1981	Grimm's second search for the ship also fails.
1983	Grimm's third search for the *Titanic* is unsuccessful.
1985	In September, with French assistance, Doctor Robert Ballard of Woods Hole Oceanographic Institute in the US discovers the wreck of the *Titanic,* in an area of the North Atlantic called the Grand Banks, some 2½ miles below the surface. The ship is found to be in two sections. Ballard brings up haunting photographic images of the ship.
1986	The definitive *Titanic* book, *Titanic: Triumph and Tragedy,* is produced by John R Eaton and Charles Haas. *The National Geographic* publishes *Secrets of the Titanic,* which includes exclusive coverage of Ballard's exploration.
1987	The French dive to the wreck and raise nearly nine hundred artefacts. The US Congress moves to try to make the *Titanic* an international memorial site.
1989	Dr Robert Ballard's *The Discovery of the Titanic* is published. The book gives a comprehensive insight into the search for and the physical state of the *Titanic.*
1991	Frank J. Goldsmith's *Echoes in the Night* is published; it includes his recollections of travelling on the *Titanic* as a third-class passenger.
	RMS Titanic Inc., the salvers in possession, started

156

to tour the world with their exhibition of artefacts raised from the wreck site. At time of writing it is estimated that over 16 million people world wide have visited the exhibition.

1992 The Ulster Titanic Society is formed in Belfast. Don Lynch and Ken Marschall publish the lavishly illustrated book *Titanic —An Illustrated History.* Film footage of the wreck is released by the IMAX film company.

1993 The company RMS Titanic Inc., formed by George Tulloch, is given salvage rights to the *Titanic* by an American court.
A report by US marine experts sparks debate regarding the quality of the steel used in the construction of the *Titanic.* Today this issue is still the topic of much heated discussion and controversy.

1994 In October, the National Maritime Museum, in Greenwich, puts on a display of the artefacts raised from the wreck by George Tulloch.

1994 *Shadow of the Titanic* — the autobiography of Eva Hart, who, as a child of seven, travelled on board the *Titanic* as a second-class passenger is published.

1996 Production work begins on a new film called *Titanic,* directed by James Cameron.
RMS Titanic Inc. begins selling coal brought up from the wreck site. RMS Titanic Inc. attempts to raise a major section of the ship's hull, but fails when a lift bag fails a few metres from the surface.

1997 The memoirs of *Titanic* stewardess Violet Jessop, who also served on the *Olympic* and the *Britannic,* are recorded in the book *Titanic Survivor: The Memoirs of Violet Jessop.*
'The Sinking of *SS Titanic*', an investigative booklet which details how and why the ship sank, is published in Belfast by Chris Hackett and John Bedford.
Father Browne's Titanic Album is published, containing unique photographs of the liner and her passengers. It becomes a bestseller in Ireland and the US (where it is titled *The Last Days of the Titanic*), and editions are sold to France, Hungary and Japan.

1998 Cameron's film *Titanic* is released and becomes the highest-grossing film ever made.
In August, RMS Titanic Inc. recovers a large section of the hull of the ship from the sea bed. It is reported that the 'big piece' is to undergo scientific tests on the steel, and then form the centre-piece of their *Titanic* exhibition.
In October, James Cameron's film *Titanic* is released on video.
Titanic Quarter Limited is established. Its aim is to regenerate the area that will later be known as Titanic Quarter.

1999 The Northern Ireland Science Park was founded by the University of Ulster, Queens University Belfast and members of the business community. It is to be established in the area adjacent to and including the Thompson and Alexandra Dry Docks as well as the Pump House.

2000 The 185-acre site of the former Harland and Wolff shipyard is now named Titanic Quarter.

2001 The Belfast Titanic Society in their magazine CQD Titanic call upon local government to purchase the tender *SS Nomadic* (the last surviving White Star ship, built by Harland and Wolff).

July New Yorkers David Leibowitz and Kimberley Miller descend to Titanic in a submersible and marry while hovering over the bow of the ship.

2002 In April, Belfast City Council hosts the first annual Titanic Made in Belfast Festival.
In May, Walter Lord, author of *A Night to Remember* and *The Night Lives On,* dies at eighty-seven years of age in New York.

2003 The Harland and Wolff shipyard launch ship number 1742 *Anvil Point,* a roll on roll off ship for the Ministry of Defence. It is felt that this is the last ship that will be built at the east Belfast shipyard.

2004 William McQuitty,the Bangor born producer of the film *A Night to Remember,* dies at his home in England aged ninety-nine.

2005 Initial proposals from a consortium are put forward for the *Titanic* Signature Project on Queens Island.

2006 In January, *SS Nomadic* is bought at auction in France by the Department of Social Development, a department of the Northern Ireland Assembly.
In March, F. John Parkinson, the spritely ninety-nine-year-old President of the Belfast Titanic Society, who saw the ship as a child, dies in Belfast.
In May, the refurbished bronze bust of Viscount William Pirrie is relocated to the grounds of Belfast City Hall following vandal attacks at the Belfast City graveyard.
In July, *SS Nomadic* returns to Belfast onboard a marine barge where the vessel is welcomed by Social Development Minister David Hanson MP and the Deputy Lord Mayor of the City of Belfast, Councillor Ruth Patterson. The vessel is moored at Queens Quay and opened for public viewing.
In December, the Department for Social Development establish the Nomadic Charitable Trust, to oversee the full restoration of *SS Nomadic* in time for the 2012 anniversary.

2007 Proposals are put forward by Titanic Quarter Limited for the Titanic Signature Project on Queens Island, that will include apartments, a hotel, a marina and the Iconic Titanic building.

2009 On the 31st of May, Millvina Dean, the last survivor of the Titanic, dies aged ninety-seven in a Nursing home in England.
In August, *SS Nomadic* is moved to a permanent position in the Hamilton Dry Dock at the Abercorn basin. Work continues on the restoration of the vessel.
Work commences on the 97 million pound Titanic Signature project. This iconic building, which overlooks the slipway where the ship was constructed, will be a Titanic tourist attraction.

2010 Apartments called the Arc and a hotel open at the Abercorn Basin.
It is announced that Belfast Metropolitian College and the Public Record Office for N. Ireland are to relocate in Titanic Quarter.

2011 Planning permission is granted to turn the former Harland and Wolff Headquarters into a 111 bedroom boutique hotel.
There are now many Titanic Societies based around the world, each looking at the disaster from their own country's perspective.

Notes to Chapters

Chapter 1

1 Interview with E. Coghlan, Chairman, Irish *Titanic* Historical Society, 16 June 1994.

Chapter 2

1 Jefferson, H., *Viscount Pirrie of Belfast,* Mullan, 1948, p. 203.
2 PRONI, Harland and Wolff records, document number D2805/TUR/44.
3. PRONI Harland & Wolff Records document number D2805/Ship/3.
4 Interview with G. Roberts, 3 June 1997.
5 Correspondence —W. McClean, 30 January 1996.
6 Correspondence — B. Millar, 28 February 1998.
7 H.M. Government *Titanic* Inquiry, question number 21269.

Chapter 3

1 Jefferson, H., *Viscount Pirrie of Belfast,* Mullan, 1948, p. 69.
2 *The Belfast Newsletter,* 3 April 1911,

Chapter 4

1 Lord, W., *The Night Lives On,* Viking, 1987, p. 21.
2 PRONI, Harland and Wolff records, document number D2805/C1/1.
3 Ibid.
4 Ibid.

Chapter 5

1 PRONI, Harland and Wolff records, document number D2805/Mm/A/l,
2 *The Irish News,* 1 June 1911 (library).
3 *The Belfast Newsletter,* 1 June 1911.

Chapter 6

1 Interview with T. McBride, 10 October 1995.

Chapter 7

1 PRONI, Articles of Agreement, document number TRANS 2A/45 381, A, B & C.
2 Ibid.

Chapter 8

1 PRONI, Harland and Wolff records, document number D2805/MIN/A/1.
2 PRONI, Harland and Wolff records, document number D2805/TUR/44.
3 Interview with J. Thompson Jr, 10 June 1994.

Chapter 9

1 *The Belfast Newsletter,* 2 May 1912.

Chapter 10

1 *The Belfast Newsletter,* 4 May 1912.
2 *The Belfast Newsletter,* 28 June 1920.
3 Ibid.

Chapter 11

1 Bulloch, S.R, *Thomas Andrews, Shipbuilder,* Maunsel, 1912, Appendix.
2 *Belfast Telegraph,* 20 April 1912.
3 *The Newtownards Chronicle,* 20 April 1912.
4 Original document, Andrews collection.
5 PRONI, Harland and Wolff records, document number D2805/HIST/5.
6 Ibid.
7 *Belfast Telegraph,* 15 April 1913.
8 Ibid.
9 *Belfast Telegraph,* 17 April 1912.
10 Interview with A. McCambley, 3 June 1995.
11 Gracie, Colonel A., *Titanic, A Survivor's Story,* Belfast: Blackstaff Press, 1991, p. 90.
12 *Belfast Telegraph,* 24 April 1912.
13 Ibid.
14 *The Belfast Newsletter,* 24 April 1912.
15 *Belfast Telegraph,* 24 April 1912.
16 *CQD Titanic,* Official Journal of the Ulster Titanic Society, Vol. 1, No.l, pp. 10-11.
17 Interview with M. McCormack, 19 November 1993.
18 *CQD Titanic,* vol. 1, no.l, p. 11.
19 Gracie, Colonel A., *Titanic, A Survivor's Story,* Belfast: Blackstaff Press, 1991, p. 90.
20 'Sent from God', Harper Memorial Baptist Church, 1972, p. 9.
21 Ibid, p. 10.
22 Correspondence with G. Murphy, March 1997.
23 PRO, Halifax, Nova Scotia, document, 'Bodies and effects recovered by *Mackey Bennett'*.
24 *CQD Titanic,* vol. 1, no.l, pp. 12-13.
25 *The Constitution* (reprinted in *The Chronicle*, 31 January 1998).
26 Copy of original document, Dornan collection; interview with K. Dornan, January 1998.
27 Ibid.
28 Ibid.
29 Ibid.
30 Ibid.
31 Ibid.

Chapter 13

1 Interview with M. Cornforth, 26 September 1997.
2 Interview with H. Currie, 10 November 1997.
3 Interview with B. Currie, 29 April 1994.
4 Interview with T. McBride, 9 July 1994.
5 Interview with W. McQuitty, 10 December 1996.
6 Interview with F.J. Parkinson, 19 July 1994.
7 Interview with G. Roberts, 10 August 1997.
8 Interview with E. Scott, 9 May 1998.
9 Interview with H. Williamson, 3 October 1997.

Bibliography

Books

Andrews, S., *Nine Generations,* Belfast: Isaac Andrews & Sons Ltd, 1958.

Ballard, R., *Discovery of the Titanic,* London: Hodder and Stoughton, 1987.

Bulloch, S.F., *Thomas Andrews,* Shipbuilder, Dublin: Maunsel and Company Ltd, 1912.

Davie, M., *Titanic,* London: BodleyHead, 1986.

Gracie, A., *Titanic, A Survivor's Story,* Belfast: Blackstaff Press, 1991.

Hammond, D., *Steel Chest, Nail in the Boot and the Barking Dog,* Belfast, 1986.

Hass, C. and Eaton, J.P., *Titanic, Triumph and Tragedy,* Somerset: Patrick Stephens Ltd, 1986.

H.M. Government, *Titanic, British Inquiry,* London, 1912.

Jefferson, H., *Viscount Pirrie of Belfast,* Belfast: Mullan, 1948.

Johnstone, R., *Belfast, Portraits of a City,* Barrie and Jenkins Ltd, 1990.

Lynch, D. and Marschall, K., Titanic: *An Illustrated History,* London: Hodder & Stoughton Ltd., 1992.

Lord, W., *A Night to Remember,* London: Longmans, 1956.

Lord, W., *The Night Lives On,* New York: Viking, 1987.

Moss, M. and Hume, J. R., *Shipbuilders to the World,* Belfast: Blackstaff Press, 1986.

O'Donnell, E.E., *Father Browne's Titanic Album,* Dublin: Wolfhound Press, 1997.

Journals

CQD Titanic, Official Journal of the Ulster Titanic Society, various editions.

A Tribute to the Engineering Staff, Institute of Marine Engineers, 1992.

Newspapers

The Bangor Spectator
The Belfast Newsletter
Belfast Evening Telegraph
The Daily Graphic, April 1912 edition
The Irish News
The Newtownards Chronicle
The Northern Constitution
The Coleraine Chronicle

Public Record Office for Northern Ireland

1901 Census
Harland and Wolff Records, Document numbers D2805
Articles of Agreement, Document number TRANS 2A/45 381, A, B & C
1912 Belfast Street Directory

Index

160

Liberating Log

Janice Gunner

Janice Gunner

ATTITUDE INDIGO
P U B L I C A T I O N S

About the Author

Janice Gunner started young with her sewing and embroidery, and always found it hard to throw away left-over dressmaking fabrics. Using them creatively in patchwork and quilting was the natural solution – and today her skills in dyeing, piecing and quilting have ensured her work a place in the collection of the UK Quilters Guild and in private collections in the UK, France and the USA.

In 1993 Janice was the first ever recipient of the City & Guilds First Prize Medal of Excellence for Patchwork & Quilting. In 1999 she won the Jewel Pearce Patterson Scholarship for International Quilt Teachers, awarded by Quilts Inc, and in 2008 she was awarded the Amy Emms MBE Award for services to Quilting.

Janice's first book – *Shibori for Textile Artists* (Anova/Batsford) – was published in 2006, and from 2005–2008 she was President of the Quilters Guild. Today she specialises in teaching patchwork and quilting internationally, nationally and in City and Guilds classes up to Diploma level in the UK, France and Spain.

Acknowledgements

Thank you to everyone who has helped to make this book possible:

To my family, in particular my husband David and son James for their support and technical expertise with cameras and computers! To Rosemary and Allan for their design, illustration, editing and working so hard to a very tight deadline!

To the quilters who allowed me to use examples of their work – Rosemary Muntus, Jan Williams, Maggi Birchenough, Lesley Williamson and Vivien Finch. And to all the students who have attended Log Cabin with Attitude and Curves in the Cabin workshops. I have lost count of how many there have been!

To Magie Relph and The African Fabric Shop for the Wax Prints and Indigo fabrics in the Sublime quilts, and to Oakshott Fabrics for the wonderful fabrics they produce which have been used to make Lipari Luminosity, Lipari Cushion and the Café au Lait panel. To Euro Japan Links for the indigo sashiko fabric in Sashiko Poppy and the ochre background fabric in Summer Glow and Echinacea, to Worn & Washed for the recycled shirt fabrics used in Escape from the City & City Shirts, and to Ann and Darren Mayner at Quiltessential.

To Connie Gilham, for the retro flower print Marsh Quilters challenge fabric used in Daisy Dots; I even used fabrics from my stash which I have had for at least 36 years for this one!

To Karin Hellaby of Quilters Haven for her advice; and encouragement and finally to all the friends and colleagues I have made and worked with in The Quilters' Guild of The British Isles.

For web links please visit me at www.janicegunner.co.uk.

Next page, top: Detail of Sublime *(52 cm square) Bottom:* Blue Green Sea *(34 cm square)*

Dedicated to Mum, who got me started with sewing when I was five. I've not stopped since!

First published by
Attitude Indigo Publications in 2010
Copyright © Janice Gunner 2010

Graphics by Rosemary Muntus
Layout by Allan Scott
Photography by David Gunner

Printed by The Midas Press plc

ISBN 978-0-9567065-0-8
Attitude Indigo Publications
44 Woodville Road, Leytonstone
London E11 3BH, UK

Tel: +44 (0)20 8989 8879
www.janicegunner.co.uk

Introduction

Log Cabin has always been one of my favourite patchwork techniques. Traditional Log Cabin uses straight logs cut from single pieces of material, often building up the patterns with light and dark colours. After many years playing with these traditional styles, I decided it was time to experiment. What would happen if I used the log cabin format, but changed it to a more contemporary design?

I devised the technique for my award winning series of *Skye Escape* quilts made between 1998–2000, and it soon turned into a very popular workshop. Today it's something of a trade mark for me. For a while it was known as 'Chop and Go, Crazy Log Cabin' – which didn't really express its true nature – so in 2001 I renamed it 'Log Cabin with Attitude'. It's still my most popular workshop.

Since then I've refined the technique and taken it in a new direction with curved seam piecing – which I call 'Curves in the Cabin'. The added bonus of both techniques is that you can use an exciting and varied selection of fabrics in the blocks – more, in fact, than you would normally use in the traditional technique.

What makes a liberated log cabin?

There are three elements that give these blocks their 'attitude' – and make them so different from traditional log cabin designs.

- First, and most distinctive, you'll notice the strip-pieced logs on the fourth round of the log cabin-style block. These are formed from a newly created fabric made from wedge-shaped strips, and cut at different widths to give the block interest.

- Secondly, there's the way each set of strips sewn around the centre shape is cut at an angle after piecing — or curved *before* piecing to give the block movement.

- And finally there's the way you put the completed blocks together!

Curves in the Cabin is all about the way you cut the shape of the curves as you work. Gentle curves will give a soft flowing look, while daring, curvaceous cutting will give the finished block a lively, wobbly look.

Both versions of the technique are machine pieced, but either can be hand- or machine-quilted. I like to machine quilt using free-motion stitching with designs such as spirals, scribble quilting, bubbles or vermicelli, but sometimes I adapt the stitching as I go. The curvy shapes work to break up the geometric lines in the piecing.

Quilting with a 'walking foot' gives a more geometric look and is also very effective, especially for beginners to machine quilting. If I'm hand quilting I love the look of big, 'sashiko' style stitches – they seem a better fit with the contemporary look of the piecing, and (if you wish) you can make them a feature by using a contrast colour thread.

Finishing your piece appropriately is one of the most important aspects of the work. Don't skimp on this: take your time and think carefully, as it will enhance the finished item. 'Don't spoil the ship for a ha'p'orth of tar.'

For quilts I use a standard binding technique, though out of preference and to fit in with the contemporary look, I use a faced binding. For wall hangings, textile art and smaller items such as place mats or table runners I use a corded edge, attaching a toning colour cording material (often cotton knitting yarn or ribbon) with a matching thread and zig-zag stitch.

There are no limits to what you can go on to do with the basic techniques. Just let your imagination flow and see what it brings!

Flowers, buildings, distant views, rusty walls and cable drums all provide inspiration. Collecting and analysing such pictures will enable you to create quilts with drama, excitement and subtlety

Colour and inspiration...

Every project needs a base from which to start – an inspiration that will set you on the right path for choosing your colour scheme and your fabrics.

Sometimes the inspiration will be one particular fabric: its pattern, perhaps, or the colour range in which it's available. But the trigger is often something else. I'm fascinated by the textures and shapes you can see in architecture, water, flowers, lichens, antique textiles and the work of many artists.

Above all, colour sets my creative juices flowing. I love it, and as a starting point for my work – whatever technique I've chosen – I like to use my own photographs, magazine cuttings, pictures in books or postcards of places I have visited. Colour helps you to start thinking in a more abstract way, taking out the elements that really speak to you and making something from them.

It was a single fabric that inspired the colours used in Klimt Curves (72 cm square) but I added lime to give zing...

Colour theory

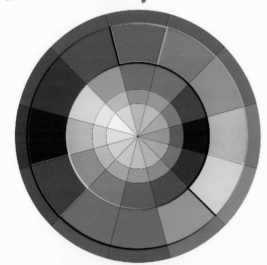

The colour wheel helps decide what colours go together. Few quilts use the pure primaries (red, blue and yellow) but many use small amounts of the opposite (or complementary) colour to give a quilt 'zing'. Paler related tints and darker shades can all give added interest.

Red, Yellow and Blue are the three *primary* colours and can be mixed to give *secondary* colours, Orange (Red + Yellow), Green (Blue + Yellow) and Purple (Blue + Red). These can be arranged on a colour wheel with intermediate (*tertiary*) colours between.

Complementary colours are those on opposite sides of the colour wheel: the complementary of Red is Green, of Yellow is Purple and of Blue is Orange.

Pure complementary hues set side by side can be too dramatic, so in a complementary colour scheme it's best to use more of one colour than the other. So if using predominantly red, add green sparingly (as an accent colour) and so on.

Tints are formed when the hue is diluted with white, and are often seen as easier to mix than pure colours. Similarly shades of the hues (where black has been added) can make for subtle colour combinations, but will always benefit from some lighter, brighter contrast colours.

Some schemes use a range of colours that are close to one another on the wheel — *analogous* colours. Others use not the only the complementary colour but those on either side of it. Thus purple can be teamed with tangerine, lemon and lime.

Colour exercise

A colour scheme based on complementary red and green adds yellow 'zing' and deep shades of red to avoid a 'Christmassy' look.

Choose an inspiration picture of your own. Take a piece of white card or paper and cut a 2" x 3" (5 x 7.5 cm) rectangle in the centre to make a viewing window. Place this over the image, moving it until you like what you see. Tape it in place if necessary.

Make a note of all the colours you see through the window, using coloured pencils if you wish. There will be more than you thought...!

Does a particular colour really sing out? If so it could be your 'zing' colour. Use it by all means, but only in a small amount or it will dominate the finished piece. (More of that later!)

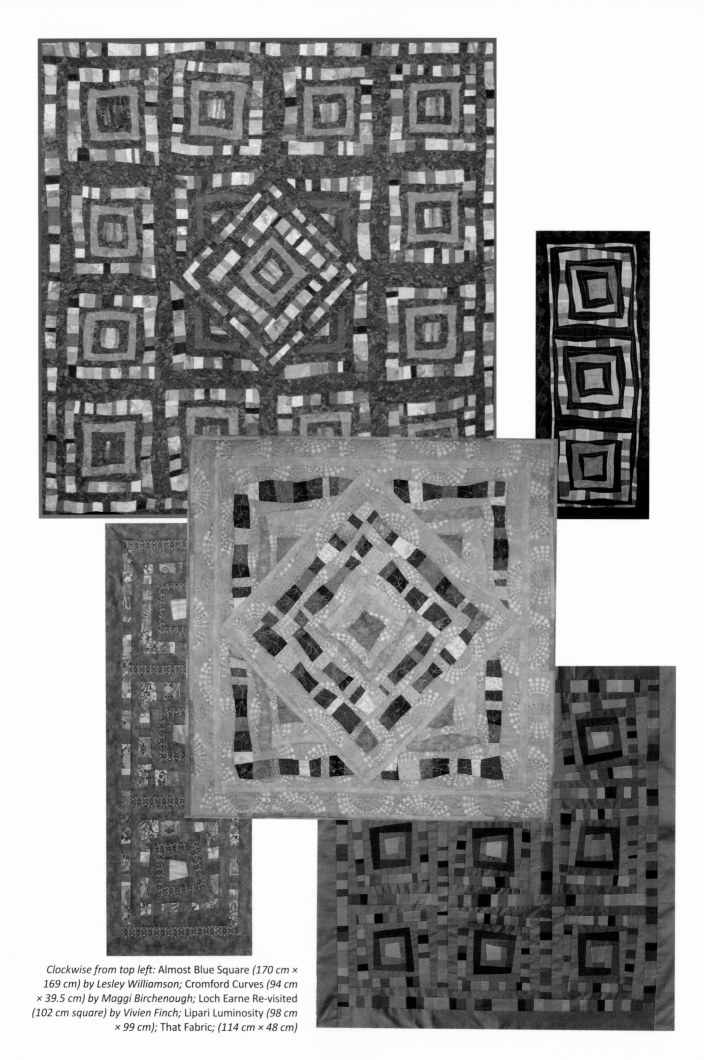

Clockwise from top left: Almost Blue Square *(170 cm ×
169 cm) by Lesley Williamson;* Cromford Curves *(94 cm
× 39.5 cm) by Maggi Birchenough;* Loch Earne Re-visited
(102 cm square) by Vivien Finch; Lipari Luminosity *(98 cm
× 99 cm);* That Fabric; *(114 cm × 48 cm)*

Getting started: 1

The colour scheme for Papaver (left, 84 cm square) was based on the predominant colours in the poppy picture above.

Gather the equipment you need

A rotary cutter, cutting mat and rulers are absolutely essential. I personally use Omnigrid/Omnigrip ruler but you will need a long one for strip cutting plus a 12–15" (30–38 cm or nearest size) square

Sewing machine and accessories: make sure your machine is in good condition, particularly if you plan to machine quilt. Make sure, too, that you have the feet you'll need for the project: a ¼" foot, a free motion foot, a walking foot and a zig-zag/cording foot (optional).

You'll need sewing kit including pins, a stitch ripper and hand sewing needles, as well as sashiko or embroidery needles if you plan to hand-quilt.

Fabric quantities

For the strip piecing (and for the even-numbered log rounds of the blocks) choose between 12 and 15 fabrics that blend with your chosen colour theme – you'll need at least a fat eighth of each fabric. One of these can also be used for the centre of your blocks, or you can choose an alternative fabric (again, take no less than a fat eighth).

For the 'background' – the alternating odd-numbered rounds of the blocks – select one colour which complements the strip piecing fabrics you have chosen. You'll need at least ½ metre or ½ yard.

Backing fabric and wadding will depend on the finished size of your project: I would suggest cutting at least ½ metre or ½ yard.

Threads

Toning or neutral colour cotton thread for piecing.

Machine quilting: toning or contrast threads such as cotton, rayon or polyester machine quilting threads.

Hand quilting: toning or contrast 'sashiko' thread or an equivalent such as cotton perlé, coton-á-broder or hand-dyed speciality threads.

With these amounts of fabric, after making your first block, you should have enough for a small wall hanging or one (possibly two) cushion covers.

Sashiko Poppy, unquilted
(25 cm square)

Getting Started: 2

Selecting your fabrics

Sort through your fabrics and lay them out on the table in a row, revealing about 1" (2.5 cm) of each fabric. Check to see if they 'work' and if they need an additional 'zing' fabric. Lay the background fabric(s) beside them to give an idea of how they will look together; change if necessary.

Put the background fabric and the separate centre fabric (if used) to one side. Now concentrate on the other fabrics to create the composite log material (using strip piecing).

Creating composite logs

1 Begin by cutting two wedge-shaped strips freehand from each of the fabrics. For speed, work without your ruler if you dare, taking care not to cut yourself. Don't worry if the strips wobble off a bit!

If you feel you need a ruler, just use it as a straight edge (without measuring) to cut your strips.

2 Make each strip narrow at one end, increasing the width as you cut towards the other end. Remember that you need to include a seam allowance, so don't cut the narrow end less than ¾" (2 cm).

Cut the fabric across from the selvedge to the cut edge; this will give you a piece approximately 20" (56 cm) long.

Tip

If you wish, you can fold the fat quarters in half to cut your strips, then cut through the fold afterwards to make two pieces from each strip. This will give you shorter strips to work with, but the effect will be the same.

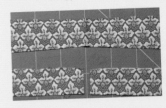

3 Cut strips from each fabric — I find it helpful to cut the narrow end approx. 1" (2.5 cm) wide, increasing to 2" (5 cm) wide at the other end as the maximum width.

4 Sort the cut strips into two separate piles. Each pile should have one strip of each colour.

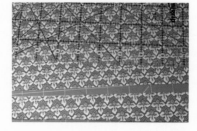

Tip

I prefer to cut each fabric individually so I can ensure a variety of different widths. If you wish you can cut through several layers of fabric at a time, though the width of the strips will be more even.

Golden Rule

Set your sewing machine stitch length to 2, which is rather shorter than usual, as you'll be cutting through the seams on this 'new' fabric later and you don't want it to unravel.

5 Begin piecing one set of these strips together in random order. Don't be tempted to 'colourwash' or graduate the colours, at this stage (I'll discuss other options later). Mix them up to make it more exciting. Take one narrow end and place right sides together against the wide end of the second piece. Then stitch, taking approx. ¼" (6 mm) seam.

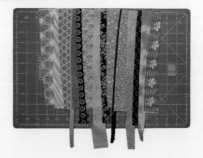

Tip

Cut 'zing' or highlight colour strips no more than 1" (2.5 cm) wide along the whole length or they will be too dominant! Feeling brave? Then cut a narrow wedge shape instead of a straight strip. One side might disappear into a seam allowance, but it will give even more 'attitude' to the finished look.

Golden Rule

Don't sew two fabrics together that are very close in value; from a distance they will look like a big chunk of the same colour – not good on the eye!

6 Continue stitching strips together until the first set is used up. You should have a new piece of fabric approx. 12–15" (30–38 cm) wide. If it's too narrow, you cut your strips too narrow to start with – so just add a few more strips to bring it up to size. If it's over 15" (38 cm), don't worry, and don't unpick!

Tip!

Rather than using the edge of the fabric as a guide (it might be a bit wobbly!) use the edge of your ¼" (6 mm) sewing machine foot. If necessary, change your needle position to get the correct seam allowance.

Golden Rule

If your fabric strips are different lengths, just line them up along the edge where you start stitching. You can even them up by cutting later, and re-use the excess. Because the strips are wedge-shaped you don't need to alternate the end where you begin stitching when adding each new strip.

7 Press all the seams in one direction, from both the back and front of the work.

Repeat stage two for the other set of strips, but remember to piece these in a different order to the first. This will ensure there is plenty of variety in the completed block. If you make them all the same the blocks will become repetitive and you'll miss out on some of that attitude!

Lay one of the strip-pieced fabric lengths on your cutting mat – and prepare to be very brave! Using your ruler, cut the strip-pieced fabric into 2" (5 cm) wide strips. Repeat with the other piece. Leave these new strips of fabric to one side for now.

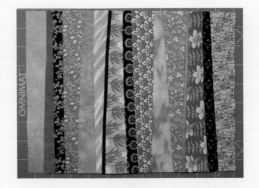

Log Cabin with Attitude

Constructing the blocks

Examples of blocks showing different background colours

For most projects you need several 3" (7.5 cm) squares to make your centres, at least two ruler-cut strips of background fabric (1½–2"; 3.75–5 cm) wide and your pieced composite logs, created using the strip-piecing techniques on the previous page.

Golden Rule

Don't cut the angles too sharply or you will have difficulty piecing the block later – it will turn out kite-shaped!

1 Take one of your 3" (7.5 cm) wide squares for the centre of each block. Trim it freehand, taking a small wedge shape off each side to produce a quadrilateral (or what I call a wonky square!)

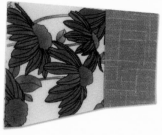

2 **First round:** take a strip of the background fabric and piece it, log-cabin style, around the centre shape. Remember, you may need extra length to allow for the angles of your centre shape before you start to stitch.

Press each seam away from the centre (finger pressing will do at this stage) and don't worry if it's uneven. And yes, I said 'log-cabin style' – so don't get too stressed out if you forget which way around the block you are going. It'll look fine, I promise!

3 Place the block on the cutting mat when you've completed the four sides of the centre shape. Using your ruler as a straight edge, trim the block – each side should become wedge-shaped.

I call this stage 're-aligning', because you can now cut the sides to make the block move in a different direction (if necessary) and give yourself a 'straight edge' to sew the next strips on to.

This example shows two different fabrics, as in variant b)

4 **Second round:** this will be made with some of the left-over fabric from your strip piecing, and there are several combinations you could try:

a) The same fabric all the way round (on all four sides)
b) Two different fabrics, placed on adjacent sides
c) 4 different fabrics, one for each side
d) a new set of fabrics that tone or complement the first choices

Whatever your choice, don't use a very dominant colour and especially not your 'zing' fabric, or it will be much too prominent. Piece these strips on to the block in the same way as step 2 and then re-align as in step 3.

5 **Third round:** repeat steps 2 and 3.

Tip!

Either look through the ruler at the shape of the fabric strip or place the ruler on the outside edge so you can see the rest of the block. Don't cut the new edge using the seam you've already stitched as a guide. It will be parallel, and we're looking for 'attitude'! The trimmed block should have a wedge shape on each of the four sides.

6 **Fourth round:** add the strip-pieced fabric around the block.

Note: you will probably have a longer length of strip-pieced fabric than you need. This gives you the chance to 'audition' it so you get the best choice of colours on each edge. If a colour is too strong, take it out, or give it a friend by unpicking the short seam and inserting another colour.

Tip!

Try to place the strip-pieced fabric so your eye is taken around the block. Don't have each side the same, and try to avoid having a prominent piece of fabric in the same place on each side of the block (although sometimes this can be an advantage)!

Golden Rule

When pressing *any* round that includes pieced strips, press the seams away from the pieced strip and towards the background strips. This avoids having too much bulk from all those extra seams.

7 **Fifth round:** repeat step 2 using 'background' fabric. At this stage I sometimes cut a wider strip of fabric (3" or 7.5 cm) to allow for squaring up the block later. Press seam away from strip-pieced fabric.

8 **Repeat step 3:** you can now 'square up' the final edges. Use your ruler, making sure of right angles at the corners if you wish!

If you've kept to the measurements given here your finished block should end up between 10–12" (25–30 cm) square.

Alternatively leave the final cutting and squaring up until all the blocks for the project have been completed, to ensure they all have the same dimensions.

9 Continue making blocks in this way until you have completed the number you need for your project.

Curves in the Cabin

This exciting variation on the previous technique came about when I was experimenting with free-cut curved piecing for a new quilt I was making.

I began to wonder if the technique would work on the strip-pieced fabric I used for Log Cabin with Attitude. I dabbled for a while and hey presto, it worked. Now the blocks really do wobble!

I was introduced to the free cut curves method by Ricky Tims but quickly realised I had known how to do it all along, only I had always associated it with dressmaking skills I learnt years before I took up quilting.

The basic technique for making a block is the exactly the same as Log Cabin with Attitude, except you are cutting curves instead of straight edges. Here's how you proceed...

Constructing the block

1 Cut 3" (7.5 cm) squares (again approximately) of your centre fabric(s).

2 Now cut a gentle curve along the first side. Don't cut too deeply, or you will have problems handling the small piece of fabric!

Tip!

A small rotary cutter makes the first few stages of this technique easier – you can move on to a standard size rotary cutter from stage 8.

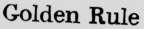

Golden Rule

Don't cut the curves too deeply or you will have difficulty piecing!

3 Start piecing the first round of the block by taking a strip of the 'background' fabric. As before, you will need two strips of this fabric cut using a ruler 1½–2" (3.75–5 cm) wide. Overlap the curved edge of the centre shape by ½"(1.25 cm) over the long edge of the strip. Both fabrics should be right side up, not right sides together!

4 Cut the strip flush with the centre shape at the top. Now, using the curve as a template, cut along that edge with your rotary cutter carefully.

Remove the narrow scrap of background strip from underneath the centre shape. Your two pieces should fit together like a jigsaw.

5 Now flip the background strip right sides together on top of the centre shape. The curved edges will look as though they don't match!

You may want to put a pin through both layers of fabric at any junctions where the two fabrics meet in the curve (though I prefer to work *without* pins). You should now be able to manipulate the fabric along the rest of the curve.

6 Stitch the pieces together with a ⅛" (3 mm) seam allowance, making sure both fabrics lie exactly on top of each other on the raw edges of the curve.

Stitch slowly, a few stitches at a time, and remember to set the 'needle down' position on your machine so it will always stop in the fabric. (Turn the balance wheel if you don't have this facility). This helps prevent the fabric from moving as you manipulate it to stitch, and also ensures you don't have to clip the seam allowance.

Press the seam to one side, away from the centre, using steam if possible.

7 Continue in this way on the other three sides of the centre shape. Always cut one side at a time as you may distort the fabric as you handle it otherwise.

8 **Second round:** this round of strips are sewn on to the block are made up from some of the remaining fabric that you cut your strip piecing from. There are several combinations that you could try, these are:

   a)   Same fabric all the way round

   b)   Two different fabrics, placed on adjacent sides

   c)   different fabrics, one for each side

   d)   a new set of fabrics that tone or complement the first choices.

Whichever choice you make, do not use a very dominant fabric, particularly your 'zing' fabric if you have one as it will be too much for the eye to focus on!

Cut the curve in the opposite direction from the first edge of the block. This will give the block movement, and make it more interesting.

You have to train your brain here. Your natural instinct will be to cut the same curve as before, but we want to give the curves 'attitude'. And that's not instinctive (or at least, not yet!)

9 Piece each strip in turn on a newly cut curved edge on the block, just as you did in steps 4–7.

10 Third round: repeat steps 4–7.

Tip!

Are you daring enough to cut really skinny curves? Try it — you only have to remember to include your seam allowance, and you'll get some really lively movement in the block!

11 **Fourth round:** now add the strip-pieced fabric around the block. Repeat steps 4–7.

Note: you will probably have a longer length of strip-pieced fabric than you need. This is so you can 'audition' it to get the best choice of colours on each edge.

If a colour is too strong, take it out (or give it a friend by unpicking the short seam and inserting another colour).

Try to place the strip-pieced fabric so your eye is taken around the block. Don't make each side the same and *do* try to avoid having a prominent piece of fabric in the same place on each side of the block (though to be fair, this can sometimes work to your advantage...)

Golden Rule

When pressing *any* round that includes pieced strips, press the seams away from the pieced strip and towards the background strips. This avoids having too much bulk from all those extra seams.

Golden Rule

Place the seams uppermost and facing towards you when stitching the composite logs. Handle the fabric very gently to prevent the stitches unravelling.

12 Fifth round: repeat steps 4–7 using 'background' fabric. Steam press the seam back towards the centre this time.

At this stage I sometimes cut a wider strip of fabric (3" or 7.5 cm) to allow for 'squaring' the block up later. Using steam, press the seam away from the strip-pieced fabric.

13 You may now 'square up' the final edges. Use your ruler to do this, making sure of right angles at the corners if you wish!

If you have kept to the measurements given your finished block should end up between 10" and 12" square. Alternatively, leave the final cutting and squaring up until all the blocks for the project have been completed, which will help to ensure they're all the same size.

14 Continue making blocks in this way until you've completed the number you need for your project.

Developing these techniques further

Experiment with fabric choices

- What about silk? (But don't forget it frays easily!)

- Using hand dyed fabrics — I love Shibori!

- Add drama with African prints, batiks etc.

- Those variegated fabrics (Moda Marbles, Fossil Ferns, Oakshott fabrics etc) create lively results.

- Consider using two contrasting fabrics for the 'background' fabrics and making several blocks from each.

- If you start to run out of fabric introduce new fabrics while you still have some of the original fabrics left. But don't panic – just make sure you balance the new fabric through several blocks.

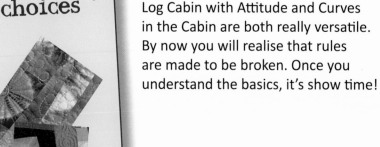

Log Cabin with Attitude and Curves in the Cabin are both really versatile. By now you will realise that rules are made to be broken. Once you understand the basics, it's show time!

Develop new strip-piecing skills

- Think about adding narrow tucks of contrast colour fabric into some of the seams as you stitch them together. This could be your 'zing', or a new colour. This technique can be used to add texture.

- Experiment with 'colour-washing' the fabrics you have chosen, or graduating them from light to dark. Although these can be effective, they will make each block fairly predictable as the same colours may end up in similar positions.

- Consider adding narrow strips of raw edge fabric into the seams for an extra tactile touch. Linen and silk are good for this.

- Experiment with inserting sheer fabrics into the seams to give shadow effects.

- What about having extra 'attitude' by making the wrong side of the strip piecing the right side when constructing the block?

Cut down waste!

- Make some smaller blocks with left-overs — remember you will need to adjust the width of the strips in both the strip pieced fabric and the blocks and take smaller seam allowance if necessary.

- Save all the cut-off pieces from the strip-pieced fabric to use for sashing the blocks, inserts or borders. They can easily be re-pieced!

Rethink block construction

- Insert tucks or raw edged strips or shapes of fabric into the some seams for extra texture.

- Consider twisting tucks at seam junctions to highlight the tuck even more.

- If you have used tucks in between the strip-pieced fabric, consider twisting these too.

- Try inserting sheer fabric between the seams as mentioned in Strip Piecing variations.

- Use a different colour fabric or specific motifs for the centre of each block.

- Vary the shape of the centre of the block — what would it look like as a triangle?

- Include a change of 'background' fabric in one of the rounds on some blocks.

- Consider adding in narrow strips of fabric between the rounds of 'background' fabric and strips or strip piecing.

- Insert 'prairie points' into the seams here and there during the construction of the block.

Daisy Dots *(50 cm square) 2010 — an example of a four-block project using Curves in the Cabin*

16

Quilt Layouts, designs and projects 1

Adapt these projects as you wish, or experiment with your own designs and alternative layouts.

One-block projects

Use individual blocks or experimental pieces to create mats, cushion covers or bags. Add additional rows of logs of either the background or the composite material to make the block large enough for your project. Layer your block with wadding and a backing and quilt.

For a small mat, simply finish with a binding or corded edge. Place mats can either be square or rectangular. Blocks will need extra borders on two sides for rectangles or alternatively construct each block with a more rectangular quadrilateral in centre to start with.

If making a cushion, the cover should be at least 1" (2.5 cm) smaller than the cushion pad to make a nice plump cushion. Layer with wadding and a backing and quilt. Construct the back from two pieces of hemmed fabric that overlap by at least 5" (12.5 cm).

Place these overlapping and face down on the front of the quilted patchwork square. Stitch all the way round, taking one or two stitches on the diagonal as you reach each corner. Trim away excess wadding at corners and zig-zag or over-lock all seams together on the outer edge to prevent wear. Turn cushion cover right side out and insert the cushion pad.

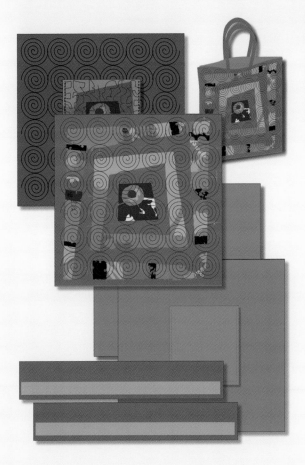

One of the easiest of bags to make, needs one large block fully quilted plus a quilted square of background fabric of the same size for the back (12–15"; 30–40 cm). You also need two further squares of lining fabric plus extra pieces for any pockets you need, and for the handles. (The back and the pockets can also be log-blocks). Finally you need two padded handles that use up the thin strips of wadding that most quilters have.

- Finish off any pockets by turning in ½" (1.25 cm) around three sides and ironing these in position. Hem the fourth side. Sew securely onto a back or a lining piece.

- Create handles from a narrow rectangle of wadding the same length as your handle. Cover this with fabric and sew several parallel rows of stitching to hold everything in place.

- Sew the quilted front and back together along the sides and the bottom. Turn right side out. Pin the handles, loops facing downwards, on the right sides of this bag.

- Sew the two lining pieces together, but leave a generous gap along the bottom edge.

- Carefully place the bag, still right sides out, inside the lining (still inside out). Line up the side seams.

- Reposition the pins holding the handles in place, and sew around the top a couple of times.

- Turn right side out and sew up the lining.

Three- or four-block projects

A bigger, better cushion or mat – using additional borders and corners

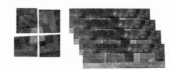
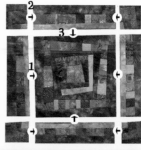
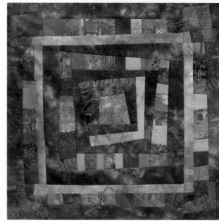

- Make a second block to round three only and cut the block through the middle each way to give 4 pieces.

- Make four border pieces – one for each side of the first block using one straight strip, one pieced strip and one 'background' strip of fabric.

- Assembly Stage 1 – Stitch a completed border on two opposite sides of the first block

- Assembly Stage 2 – Join a corner piece to each end of the remaining two border pieces.

- Assembly Stage 3 – Stitch these longer borders on the other two sides. Press and trim if necessary.

Layer with wadding and backing fabric, quilt and finish off as desired.

Quirky Corners
(44 cm square)

A simple wall hanging or table runner: Take three blocks to make a long, narrow wall hanging or table runner. Add extra strips of either the composite log or background fabric to finish. Square up the blocks, sandwich strips between the blocks, before adding a final border all the way round the 'background' fabric. Layer up with wadding and a backing, and quilt and finish the edges with a binding or with a corded edge. Add a hanging sleeve if making into a wall hanging, and remember to sign and date your work.

Escape from the City *(82 cm × 27 cm)*

Purple Pleasures *(76 cm square)*
by Rosemary Muntus

A square wall hanging or large cushion cover made from four (or five) blocks.

- Choose the best of the blocks for the centre.

- Cut two of the remaining blocks in half, one vertically and the other horizontally (this may matter depending on the shape of the centre of each block).

- Cut the remaining block into four – this is where you may need a fifth block in order to get the right orientation of the block. You may need to fiddle to get the four corner pieces.

- Join the vertically cut block to either side of the centre one. Trim and add additional strips if necessary. Measure the row carefully and match this to the other cut pieces.

- Stitch a corner piece to either end of each horizontally cut block. Again trim and add strips to get things to fit if necessary.

- Join these new rows to the centre section and press.

- Trim and square up as required. Add further borders if you wish.

- Layer with wadding and a backing and quilt.

- Add a hanging sleeve if making into a wall hanging and remember to sign and date your work.

- If making a cushion complete as in the single block project.

An 'on point' design wall hanging or cushion.

- Choose the best of the three blocks for the centre. Cut the remaining two blocks through the centre diagonally and measure the hypotenuse (the cut edge).

- Add another round of strip-pieced fabric strips to the centre block, plus another round of 'background' fabric to make this block large enough.

- Trim the edges to make sure they are straight. Join the diagonal cut blocks to the centre block, stitching them on opposite sides. Press and trim up if necessary.

- Add a border all the way round if you wish using strip pieced fabric, joining to make up the required length if necessary.

- Layer with wadding and a backing and quilt. Finish edges with a binding or a corded edge.

- Add a hanging sleeve and sign and date your work.

If making a cushion complete as in the single block project on page 17.

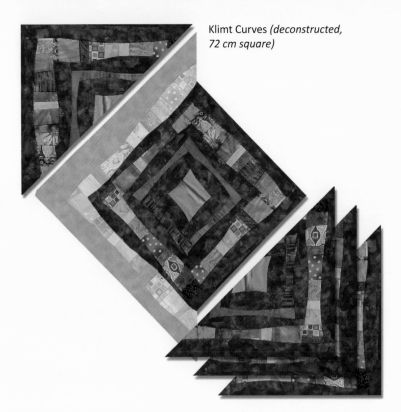

Klimt Curves *(deconstructed, 72 cm square)*

Multi-block projects

Curves in the New England Cabin
(122 cm square) by Jan Williams

Curves in the New England Cabin

- This lively design by Jan Williams is made with just seven blocks.

- Choose the best block for the centre, then cut each of the remaining blocks in half diagonally.

- Stitch the required number of borders around the centre block (Jan has used two rows each of the 'background' fabric and of strip piecing) so it becomes the same length as the hypotenuse of the triangles. Stitch a triangle to each side.

- Make four rectangular insert sections consisting of two strip pieced logs either side of one 'background' strip to the required length of the right-angle sides of the remaining triangles.

- Piece remaining triangles in pairs, with an insert section, to make four large corner triangle units. Stitch these units to the edges of the centre section of the work and trim if necessary.

- Stitch a border on each side made from the remaining strip piecing; then make a final border using background fabric with narrow strips of some of the left-over strip piecing fabrics.

- Layer the quilt top with wadding and backing fabric and quilt as desired. Bind the quilt with the remaining 'background' fabric, including some short lengths of strip piecing if you have any left. Label your quilt and add a hanging sleeve if necessary.

Quilting and finishing

Quilting

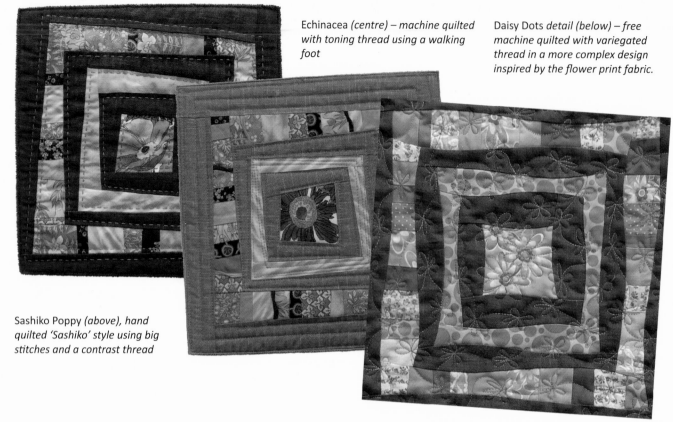

Echinacea *(centre) – machine quilted with toning thread using a walking foot*

Daisy Dots *detail (below) – free machine quilted with variegated thread in a more complex design inspired by the flower print fabric.*

Sashiko Poppy *(above), hand quilted 'Sashiko' style using big stitches and a contrast thread*

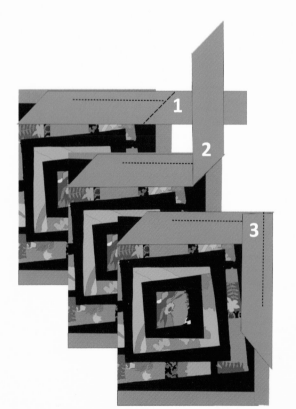

Finishing Techniques

These items were finished in several ways.

Traditional binding using a continuous bias strip or **Folded binding**, which uses a straight strip of fabric folded double.

- When you have trimmed the quilted item off, assemble a strip about 8" (20 cm) longer than the sum of all your sides. Mitre the joins.

- Start the binding in the middle of one side

- Mitre the corners by sewing almost up to the corner (1), stopping and folding at 45 degrees (2), folding back, and restarting the sewing (3).

- Hand stitch the binding at the back.

Right: Folded binding on Purple Pleasures *by Rosemary Muntus*